CHINESE ENCOUNTERS

Farrar · Straus · Giroux | New York

Wall poster "Democratic Wall," Chang An Avenue, Peking

CHINESE
ENCOUNTERS

Inge Morath | Arthur Miller

Library of Congress Cataloging in Publication Data
Morath, Inge.   /   Chinese encounters.
1. China—Description and travel—1976–
2. China—Intellectual life.
3. Miller, Arthur—Journeys—China. 4. Morath, Inge.
I. Miller, Arthur.   /   II. Title.
DS712.M67   /   951.05   /   79–13128

Grateful acknowledgment is made to the following for
permission to reprint copyrighted material: George Allen &
Unwin Ltd.: a selection from *The Book of Songs*, translated
by Arthur Waley. Doubleday & Company, Inc.:
excerpts from *Sunflower Splendor* by Wu-chi Liu and
Irving Yucheng Lo, copyright © 1975 by Wu-chi Liu and
Irving Lo. Grove Press, Inc.: excerpts from *Anthology of
Chinese Literature*, Vol. I and Vol. II, edited by Cyril Birch,
copyright © 1965, 1972 by Grove Press, Inc. Harvard University
Press, Cambridge, Mass., and Faber & Faber Ltd., London:
selections from *The Classic Anthology Defined by Confucius*,
translated by Ezra Pound, copyright 1954 by the President
and Fellows of Harvard College. Alfred A. Knopf, Inc.:
selections from *The Jade Mountain: A Chinese Anthology*,
translated by Witter Bynner from the texts of Kiang Kang-Hu,
copyright 1929 and renewed © 1957 by Alfred A. Knopf, Inc.

[*A Note on Transliteration*]

The reader of this book will note that the spelling of many of the names of Chinese people and places is somewhat unfamiliar. We have decided to adopt the new system of transliteration of Chinese characters known as Pinyin. This is the system now used by the official news agency Xinhua (Hsinhua), *The New York Times*, *Time*, and many other prominent Western newspapers and journals.

Pinyin (actually the Chinese word for transliteration) was originally devised in China in the 1950's in an effort to establish a system that conformed more closely to standard Beijing (Peking) pronunciation, and to avoid the difficulties of distinction between some sounds (such as "b" and "p") that the old Wade-Giles system creates. Since it is hard for any system to render the sounds of Chinese in the Roman alphabet, with Pinyin, too, some have had to be interpreted by letters that are a representation rather than a real approximation of the sound. For instance, "q" is now used for a "ch" sound (as in the Daqing oil field, formerly written Taching), and "x" represents the hissing sound rendered traditionally as "hs," as in Deng Xiaoping (Teng Hsiao-ping).

For some names, of course, the Pinyin and Wade-Giles system coincide, as in Shanghai, Harbin, and Hunan, and in order to retain some familiarity and spare the reader unnecessary confusion, the old spellings of Peking, Sun Yat-sen, Yangtze, and Chiang Kai-shek have been kept. China itself remains the same. But Mao Tse-tung has become Mao Zedong, and his widow, Chiang Ching, is now Jiang Qing. Some other common names that have metamorphosed into forms that for a time will look odd are:

Wade-Giles	*Pinyin*
Canton	Guangzhou
Chekiang	Zhejiang
Chou En-lai	Zhou Enlai
Hangchow	Hangzhou
Hua Kuo-feng	Hua Guofeng
Kiangsi	Jiangxi
Kuomintang	Guo Mindang
Kwangsi Chuang	Guangxi Zhuang
Kweilin	Guilin
Lin Piao	Lin Biao
Nanking	Nanjing
Szechwan	Sichuan
Sian	Xian
Tientsin	Tianjin
Tsinghua	Qinghua
Yenan	Yanan

I.M. / A.M.

A few days after our return from China I sat down to go through the mail. My desk had become slightly unfamiliar as the result of six weeks away from it. Seeing its disorder with fresh eyes, I noticed that on it were two pencil sharpeners facing each other. With some small amusement I realized that they had been there for years. One, the type that is screwed down, I had removed from the kitchen wall years ago during a renovation and had never gotten around to putting up again; the other, an "improved" model with a vacuum base which is supposed to stick anywhere but never did long enough to sharpen a pencil, I had simply abandoned there in a mood of defeated bitterness. That both devices have stood facing each other for so long in the midst of the clutter of paper is doubtless an event of several possible meanings, but none has yet occurred to me.

If a visiting foreigner—let us say a Chinese—were ever to notice them, however, he might well wonder why they were there since people always apply a logic abroad which they would never dream of using at home, and, if he were of a philosophical or sociological turn of mind, would most likely try to extrapolate from their absurd presence some theoretical insights into American life and our society. The moral, as I see it, is that no one can think he knows a country until he can easily separate its merely idiosyncratic absurdities from its real contradictions.

We do not "know" China when we still notice and are even startled by things no Chinese pays the slightest attention to. But the ability to be surprised is a virtue in a photographer, especially if like Inge Morath her eye can be caught while her mind is informed by knowledge of the Chinese language and a long familiarity with China's arts. This book, however, makes no claim to expertise; it is an encounter, after long preparation, with China in the direct or even abrupt sense of that word. For we were surprised in China by an unforeseen accident of history.

We had arrived in the fall of 1978, precisely at a moment when for the first time in thirty years people felt safe enough to talk freely to foreigners about what had been happening during the past decades. Having written about and photographed in the Soviet Union and Eastern Europe, we approached China prepared to deal with the dissimulations of a one-party society, including the usual police surveillance of our movements. It was a shock to be confronted instead by people not only willing to speak but insisting on telling about their own and others' recent sufferings under the so-called Gang of Four (which one soon learned was merely a screen for the still-sacrosanct name of Mao).

But that shock soon became a kind of spur to an inquiry which we could not have foreseen. We found ourselves among people who were just beginning to throw off both outer and inner censorship, and with the most excruciating sort of honesty, the kind that did not omit their own contributions to their plight. For myself, I had expected to observe, but I had not thought I was to be educated not merely in things Chinese but in matters of social principle which also underlie the dilemmas of American and European society.

Our interests in China, it must be said, are not quite of the same order. For Inge Morath there was initially the challenge of learning the language and adding it to the half dozen others in which she is fluent or, like Rumanian, of which she has a working knowledge. The calligraphy led her to Chinese art, and the art to history. After four intense years of study, she greeted our interpreter, Su Guang, at the Peking airport in his own language and they shared a delighted astonishment that she was being so completely understood.

For me, China had been primarily a political and social revolution I had followed since the thirties, when the names of Mao Zedong and Zhou Enlai and Zhu De were like flares shot into the sky out of a human sea, a hitherto silent mass of people suddenly defying the Japanese fascists and, surely, prophesying the dawn of reason and liberty in Asia. For a while I had had the friendship, too, of Edgar Snow, who would often stop by to pick up his soon-to-be wife, Lois Wheeler, after her performances in my play *All My Sons*. His *Red Star Over China*, the best single reportage I have ever read and surely among the most influential ever written, seemed at the time to promise a new stage of human development, a Marxist revolution whose leaders had a sense of humor, irony, and, in Zhou's case, a cultivated sensibility one had never associated with their kind in the Soviet Union.

I must admit, however, that in recent years I had all but given up hope of understanding what was happening in China. Under a barrage of factional leaders' names I could never remember, and their conflicting claims, which seemed a confused, strident, hair-splitting sectarianism, I had left Chinese politics to the Chinese. And this was just as well, I now discovered, for I arrived quite without preconceived notions on the merits of any of the arguing sides.

The China of 1978 is the pyrrhic triumph of factionalism, but of an intensity beyond the capacity of mortal mind to follow. The maze-like complexity of events, moreover, had been compounded even for the Chinese by the refusal of the press to report "negative" events, so that a devastating fight could have occurred a few miles from Peking with few who were not eyewitnesses even knowing about it. And some of these were factional battles that killed people in the tens of thousands.

What is difficult to comprehend in Chinese factionalism, apart from its sheer density, is that this traditional curse of the left could flower, cross-pollinate, wind its endless branches around the pillars of the state and pull it all crashing to the ground—while the state power itself either stood apart, merely remonstrating as Mao would from time to time, or else actually entering the fray as one of the factions itself. This is not conceivable, I suppose, in any other country. So a contradiction must be admitted, that while China's government operated as it still does in the usual secrecy of any Communist regime, it at the same time carried on a sort of yelling debate with sects and factions within it and below it in the Party to the point where strictly speaking there was no government of China—the army excepted—and the field was left to terror and brute force. To seek the nuggets of principle in these factions is probably pointless, for as William Hinton has demonstrated in his book *Hundred Day War*, the battles begun in principle to "support Mao" finally were allowed to degenerate into classical clashes of power-lusting young men whose forces often melted into each other and separated into three, four, or more subgroups, each well salted with paranoids and in the end combining only as that joyfully triumphant permanent party in human affairs which is always in love with falling stones.

Inge Morath's photographs—always drawn to the lasting, the beautiful, the evidences of history's grace—are not mere scenery here, however they may please the eye. They are in their loveliness one arm of China's contradiction—her ancientness and solemnity, which ceaselessly work against and with her epic struggle to change herself at last and become a modern nation.

But this is not a book about the Cultural Revolution and its consequences, which, like the Thirty Years' War in Europe, will be sifted by generations of scholars and made to confirm a thousand different conclusions. It is a witness, neither more nor less, of two people encountering the collapse of an orthodoxy at the very time when the faithful were emerging from the fallen temple with blinking eyes, trying to make out ordinary objects in the no longer charmed, unearthly light of ordinary days. It is the moment when the great choirs of the worshippers are stilled, when the mountains have ceased to dance (as some insist they did), and Necessity once again is deaf to all rhapsodic persuasions and will yield only to accountants and engineers, and the kind of people who may get things done but can never believe in what they cannot touch and see. And this too will pass into yet newer permutations. Here, then, is a bit of how it was for two people, well disposed and trying to see and listen, at the particular moment when the dust of the temple began to settle.

One learns soon enough that only a fool understands the Chinese quickly. Nevertheless, after two days in Qiao Yu's gentle company, his sympathetic curiosity about our American lives has deftly ripped the veil between us as citizens of two mutually isolated nations. In his forties, a poet and playwright, Qiao has a delicacy of manner that never varies through the eight hours of each day we are together. It takes some studying to realize that the look in his sadly humorous eyes, as he listens to Inge Morath reading aloud Tang poetry in Chinese, is one of deep admiration. Indeed, I find with a glance that he sometimes studies her like a visitor from another galaxy.

This morning the three of us—along with our guide, Su Guang, who is limping a bit less today after applying some American athlete's foot medicine I forced on him—are descending a broad stairway four stories down into the earth. Now we enter the gray cut-stone arched vaults, some two stories high, which for centuries concealed the treasures of the Ming emperors' tombs. Disappointingly, there is little to see here but the empty vaults themselves and one or two immense thrones of dragon-embossed stone far too heavy to move. Two dutiful young women wrapped against the dampness in black cloaks like Andalusian shepherdesses forlornly preside over the tourists and the gloom. Still, there is something awesome and imperial in the sheer weight of the stone overhead, all so carefully set in place to guard the great dead and their treasure against thieves and the Mings' political enemies. But it was a task which for an odd reason was finally left unperformed.

Qiao Yu

Out in the sunshine again I ask Qiao Yu how the recently excavated tombs happened to have been discovered. "The Emperor had left a stone," he explains, "which described their exact location and this stone was found not long ago. The general location has always been vaguely known."

Sensing an amusing paradox, I say, "He went to all that expense to keep the treasures hidden and safe, but his ego couldn't bear it that people would never be able to admire them." Both men give me startled looks and I continue, "So you were led to his tomb by his vanity."

They laugh with what seems extravagant surprise. "That is very clever!" says Qiao Yu, a man not easily driven to laughter. But his being so stirred by this fairly obvious paradox is what intrigues me. The same is happening to Su Guang, apparently—his moods by now more readable to us—and when in the next few minutes both men return to this remark of mine yet again, it seems that something more than the Emperor and his tombs is involved here.

It occurred to me, as it would again with other Chinese later on, that what they found so strange was my deducing a leader's character from his public acts. It was not that leaders are not acknowledged as having individual personalities, but that Power has none, and as Marxists, the Chinese have been trained to regard those on top purely as voices or expressions of economic and political forces, of the class struggle. That a leader's mere personal vanity could have had such grand consequences was a fundamentally inadmissible idea. Yet, that Qiao Yu and Su Guang recognized it—like some long-forgotten but welcome thought—was proved by their deeply inward laughter of recognition, the laughter of an irony enjoyably perceived. But they remain a classical people, I think; like our Aeschylean Greeks, for what still interests them most is not gossip about characters and their idiosyncrasies but rather their impact upon the public fate.

Ming tomb, Peking

But if there was a principle behind their uneasiness with this kind of psychologizing of historical events, there was also a concrete and current reason. From our first hour in China my wife and I were regaled—pelted, bathed, swabbed would be better words—with accounts of the depredations of the Gang of Four. After the initial shock it almost began to seem funny to be blaming all the ills of a country of perhaps one billion on three men and one woman, and it was difficult at first to take absolutely seriously. From the paucity of contemporary plays and films to the condition of public transport to the hermetic ignorance of any world outside China—all was the doing of this manic faction of the Central Committee, which, having seized control of the country at some strangely indeterminate time in the past, was only brought to book by the Party's then Vice Chairman, Hua Guofeng, who had arrested the vile quartet two years earlier and with his own group assumed the leadership.

Notwithstanding Soviet revilement of Trotsky, such open condemnation of even rejected leaders in a Communist country had an odd sound, especially since what Jiang Qing, Mao's wife, and her cohorts were charged with were not merely strategic errors but a personal moral rottenness which is not supposed to afflict even mistaken Marxists who have held power for so long. To hear Qiao Yu as well as other writers, directors, and actors tell it, Jiang Qing had behaved more like a bitterly vengeful aging actress than a political leader of the world's largest nation. For example, a host of Shanghai theater and movie folk were arrested in the seventies for no other reason than that they knew of her checkered past as a Shanghai actress in the thirties, when, it was believed, she had sold herself to the hated Guo Mindang secret police to work as their agent against the Communist revolutionaries.

It was turning out much as a Canadian reporter had predicted on our first day in Peking. "They're going to blame everything that's wrong with the country on the Four. At a banquet recently I sat down on a chair that collapsed, and as I hit the floor I looked out at the audience and yelled, 'Gang of Four!' They all died laughing."

Nevertheless, if only as a symbol of a tyrannical decade, the Gang of Four represented anarchy, an assault upon reason, and the cause behind the stubborn backwardness of the country. And so I asked Qiao Yu whether thought was being given at any level of the government to preventing another wild faction from seizing power in the future. And it ought to be said that Chinese now, despite a very obvious embarrassment and pain at such a question, are willing to face it—and with it the fact that they have been supinely faithful to petty tyrants, and worse yet, in the name of Scientific Marxism. But it is also true that they are nearly alone among citizens of socialist states in their willingness to discuss publicly not only the system's successes but also its crippling failures.

"Many of us are asking ourselves the same question," Qiao Yu replied.

"Do you have any answers?"

It was clear he was loath to continue but would anyway. "We thought she was speaking for Chairman Mao, you see. We did not know how sick he was in the last years of his life."

"And of course she held on to power after his death."

"Yes, she did."

"Is it difficult for you now to confront those years?"

He glanced away, then willed himself to look at me. He was embarrassed. "Yes, it is difficult."

We were cruising slowly along the sunlit surface of the shallow Kun Ming Lake at the Peking Summer Palace. Fish were leaping out of the water beside the boat. On a small table between us was a plate of apples, caramels, and orange pop provided by the Association for Friendship with Foreign Countries. We were moving parallel to a high masonry wall that had surrounded the lake four centuries ago. Indeed, at the beginning of the century the last Empress had built this private park and lake, which had nearly been snatched away from the people again by the most recent ruling lady. For Jiang Qing, incredibly, had tried to shut the park to the public—as she had two others—for use as her private preserve.

Kun Ming Lake

It was still early in our Chinese voyage and I did not yet know what I would know soon; like the French, the Chinese consider their country the center of the world, and therefore have had little interest in traveling abroad. It was always drought, flood, famine, or some other desperate circumstance, rarely curiosity, that had sent them out of China.

I asked Qiao Yu, "Do you get to see much foreign literature?"

"Yes, a little."

"Any American?"

"We have one book in the Writers' Union translated from America."

"Which is that?"

"*Jonathan Seagull*. But it is only available so far to Union members, not the public."

"That's the only recent American book translated?"

"I have also read *Love Story*. What do you think of those books?"

It was impossible to estimate from his avid but neutral expression whether he wanted a compliment on their having translated these books, or a confirmation of his own low opinion of them.

"They're all right," I said, "but we have better ones." He nodded, still neutrally. "Why were those books selected for translation, do you know?"

"Because they were so popular in America. It was thought that they would help us to understand the Americans."

"Ah."

"Yes."

"Do you feel you learned something from them?"

With a slight shrug, he blinked enigmatically at the air. "It is difficult to say, it is all so far from us."

I thought of one of the Russians' favorite American social novelists. "I suppose you have Jack London?"

"Yes. And Mark Twain."

"Hemingway?"

Qiao Yu glanced uncertainly toward Su Guang, who rendered the name for him in its Chinese pronunciation. "There was *The Old Man and the Sea* many years ago, yes."

"Faulkner, I suppose."

Su Guang now asked me to spell it and then pronounced it "Faul-ki-nuh" for Qiao Yu, who, like him, had never heard the name or Steinbeck's or, as it turned out, any other American writer's I now mentioned. In Qiao Yu's mild eyes I could see the United States floating far, far off somewhere in the vicinity of the Milky Way.

"We have Balzac."

"He's French."

"Yes."

Kun Ming Lake

But no English writers or any other foreigners or non-Soviet Russians excepting Chekhov and Tolstoy, not even Dostoevsky, although he had heard the name.

I was astounded by the hermetic insularity of this writer facing me across the soda pop and the apples and candy on this lovely afternoon until an old joke about the English passed through my mind, the one about the London newspaper headline: DENSE FOG —CONTINENT ISOLATED. How many Chinese writers did I even know the names of, free as I was to read anything? And had Qiao Yu not a better right than I to provincial sequestration when there were nearly a billion Chinese, a quarter of the human race, as against only two hundred or so million Americans? In fact, he had more compatriots than the populations of Europe, Russia, and half of India combined. Which of us was the provincial?

I thought about this for a while and decided, after all, that he was, primarily because he clearly thought so too. "We are far behind," he finally said, "we haven't enough translators yet for any of the languages, and in the last years everything foreign has been either forbidden or made to seem dangerous." But then he appeared to feel that he may have been too sweeping. "But we have just published a translation of *Peer Gynt*," he recalled.

I tried to look congratulatory. We were now drifting toward the shore where the Marble Boat stands. This structure of stone, a "marvel" conceived by the last Empress, Ci Xi, around the turn of the century, is two stories high and with its paddle wheels rather resembles a Mississippi riverboat. The Empress had paid for it with money appropriated for a navy to resist foreigners. But in a sense, she had done the right thing, for at least China had this park and the marble boat to show for money that would not have deflected the power of Japan or the West for a single week longer. Or so our poet-friend thought.

Ci Xi's Marble Boat, Summer Palace, Peking

[2]

It took about three days of intensive conversations to convince me of their nearly total ignorance of the West's culture. One always assumes, for some reason, that in a totalitarian state surely the leaders and intellectuals will not be foolishly bound by the isolation imposed on the people. In my case there was little excuse for this mistake, since Inge and I, some two years earlier, had accompanied a high Chinese foreign-service official and his wife, at his request, to a performance of a one-act play of mine in New York. At supper afterward I had experienced for the first time the blank in their awareness of the West. This diplomat, who of course was intelligent and sophisticated, had admitted that the last news they had had in China of American literature was of Dreiser and the iconized Mark Twain.

Confronting the same cultural blank inside China now, I recalled that it had taken the entire dinner before the diplomat had quietly confessed that they actually knew nothing of America at all, mainly because of our Chinese blockade. What he knew but could not add then was that the blockade was as bad or worse from the Chinese side, but Mao and his wife's coterie would have to disappear before such admissions would be possible.*

---

* Our own State Department-induced ignorance of China was of course sealed with the dismissal and disgrace in the 1950's of our few journalists and foreign-service officers who had observed the oncoming revolution from sufficiently close quarters to be tarred by their proximity to it. Our so-called McCarthy period of hysterical jingoism and engineered condemnations for non-criminal political opinion was our own analogous experience with extreme chauvinism.

The gap caused by our mutual ignorance of each other's real rather than reported culture seemed limitless one morning when we sat down to talk with some ten scenarists, movie directors, novelists, and one actress in a Peking hotel. It struck me at once that none appeared younger than forty-five and that most were over fifty. I found this discouraging; it meant, I mistakenly thought, that I was being boxed in by an older and doubtless more conservative generation of artists and that our visit, which was only just beginning, would be "official" and uninformative. And so I began by saying that as we were all artists I hoped to exchange experiences rather than official signals and that I had come to find out what I could about creative people's lives in China. Naturally no one knew where to begin after that, and, worse yet, I thought I might have offended them by implying that they intended to be less than candid.

As in any such group, one person seemed to be central, a man in his early sixties, handsome yet with a gauntness in his face that suggested physical suffering. And in fact he walked with a cane and leaned heavily on it and had dropped into one of the overstuffed armchairs with obvious relief. Each of us had a wide and deep cup of tea to sip at while Su Guang proceeded to translate for me quick autobiographical sketches of all present. From the books and plays they had written and the films they had acted in or directed, they seemed a productive and busy group of professionals. It would be a little while, however, before it was made clear that they had produced nothing for the past ten or so years and that most of them had spent some or all of that time incarcerated.

Their biographies completed, they then asked me who I was and what I had done. I had assumed at least some minimal awareness on that score, but I managed to down my embarrassment at having to put forward my credits. I felt a far more deeply depressing sense of hopelessness that such isolation could actually have been structured and maintained. But by the time I had finished reviewing my working life for them, I felt curiously at ease, as though we were all failures together and without any authority other than what we might win now as we emerged from darkness to confront each other. Surely this was better than the vying of stars, which had deformed similar séances in other places in other years.

There was indeed some sparring, but I was grateful for the absence of the false heartiness of writer delegations I had met in other socialist countries where the writer who shows up to greet foreign colleagues is either an official or is constrained to behave like one. It was the lone actress and the man with the cane who seemed especially to emanate a gravity, one might almost call it a direct message of suffering, which they made no attempt either to conceal or to dramatize. The man with the cane kept smiling faintly at me and the actress seemed to be on the edge of her chair

Jin Shan

with an open eagerness to tell me something she apparently had resolved to transmit without fail.

Out of polite deference, however, or perhaps an uncertainty as to how to deal with me, they kept their silence now. And the moment lengthened while they stared at me with expectation. I finally concluded that as the guest it was for me to set out a theme, and so I asked if they would talk about some of the problems they had as working artists. Or, I added quickly, perhaps they had no problems worth mentioning.

That produced an outburst of surprised laughter that brought us at once a long step closer. One problem was that there were practically no trained actors in China any more, or actresses or directors under sixty; the younger ones had no experience. Why this age gap? I asked naïvely. The Gang of Four, they claimed, had shut down the training schools for many years now.

At that moment—on our third day in China—I was still not sure what they really intended me to believe. Having had the experience of receiving ambiguous signals in one-party states, especially in hotel rooms such as this, where bugging is assumed, it crossed my mind now that with straight faces they were delivering the official line against the Four but at the same time making it so absurd that I would catch on to their real intention of mocking that line. This reasoning collapsed, however, when I saw in their eyes not the slightest glint of irony.

I decided to grab the bull by the horns. "Frankly, I can't understand what you're telling me. What possible reason could they have had to close down acting and directing schools?"

The man with the cane, the handsome fellow with the gaunt face and the marvelously intelligent eyes, merely smiled at me and kept his silence, even though some of the others were glancing toward him, apparently expecting him to take the floor. But he would not. Not yet. The lone actress spoke.

"She wanted to prevent the young people from becoming more famous than she." There was no stridency in her manner or voice, as though her explanation was obvious, something everyone in China understood.

"I have to tell you," I said, "that you make her seem a bit insane."

The actress nodded and like the others she smiled faintly—with embarrassment that the would-be Empress, wife of the beloved Chairman, had been off her rocker, and that she had nevertheless led a quarter of the human race and with no effective voice raised in opposition. (And of course there was also amusement at the idea of human craziness itself.) I chose not to pursue further the sheer triviality of their recent leadership, since it would inevitably put the Marxist system itself at issue, something one assumed they would not wish to discuss, especially with a foreigner.

And so for a few moments we all retreated from the tension and

Right: Zheng Zenyao; left: Jin Shan

1

someone asked how American writers get paid, a question every Chinese artist I would meet in the next weeks would manage to ask. I explained about play and book royalties, which had once existed among them too, until the Four suspended such payments in order to prevent formation of a class of well-paid writers separated by their money from the peasants and workers. Whether to reinstitute royalties was now being widely discussed and no one yet knew whether they would return. Meanwhile, each writer and director and performer received a salary from his own union, roughly fifty or sixty yuan per month, or about forty dollars. On this question they were still not certain where they stood; they too feared splitting themselves away from the general poverty of the people.

But since they were paid regularly whether or not they produced any work—as some had not for more than a decade because of a want of inspiration as well as actual incarceration—it was with a certain incredulity that they received my news that an American author did not get paid at all excepting as his work sold or was performed. Inge Morath, seeing that they were being too polite to tell me that this seemed a barbaric system, corrected me and in Chinese informed them that a Western writer could sometimes live for years on one book or play. They nodded with relief, surprisingly enough, for as I would learn later they were not looking for bad news about America. We all need something to believe in, apparently.

Meantime, through all this, my curiosity about the man with the cane kept mounting, chiefly because I had almost decided that he understood English, so changeful was the expression on his face with the shifts in my responses and questions. In a momentary hiatus I turned to him directly and asked if he were primarily a writer or a director and some little wavelet of embarrassment rippled across the company, plus a hair of pique whisking over his face, all of which of course announced his stardom and my ineptitude.

And in fact, as two of the others quickly told translator Su—who allowed himself to show a shy discomfort for having failed to inform me more precisely—Jin Shan had been since the thirties probably the greatest film star in China, as well as one of a handful of her most gifted directors, until his imprisonment for over nine years by the Gang. Moreover, while appearing to live the film star's swinging life in pre-Liberation Shanghai he had been a secret Communist and at daily risk had provided information to the Party about the political and underworld organizations that ran the city and to which he had gained entree.

I apologized to Jin for my ignorance and he immediately laughed and put me at my ease. I asked him why he had been arrested and he said simply, "I knew her in Shanghai," Jiang Qing, that is. "And also because she wished never to contend with people who had talent. Everyone you see in this room has been in prison or held in detention for two, five, eight, or nine years, and in each case it finally comes down to their talent." He did not cease smiling, nor did he say that he did not expect me to believe him or that he would try to convince me of their common experience. He was a modern man with a contemporary wit in his eyes, and he knew how insane it all sounded, but that was how it was.

I took out my notebook then and openly took down what he was saying. I asked if he carried a cane because of injuries in detention, but he simply looked at me, refusing to talk about it, and I understood. Now the actress spoke. She was sitting beside him. Turning to her, I was shocked to see tears flowing down her cheeks.

"They killed his wife, Sun Weishi," she said. "She was our greatest actress, the most beloved in all China in our lifetime. They murdered her."

"Why? Why did they do that?" It was hard to keep looking at the fury and suffering in her face.

"Because the people adored her so. She was my teacher, you see. We were very dear and close friends. They killed her in the same camp as he was, but he did not know that when he was let out. He expected to be reunited. They had killed her three years before and had never told him."

I looked at Jin Shan, who seemed to lounge in the enormous overstuffed chair, one hand resting on the arm and the other on his walking stick, and he was still smiling at me, and now I thought there was a certain challenge in his smile.

I knew how they had revered Chairman Mao, and even in our short time in China it was obvious that his memory was, or was supposed to be, sacrosanct. But the quickened arithmetic going on in my head told me that Jin had been arrested while Mao was as yet by no means incapacitated. And therefore to say what I was about to say, and felt it necessary to say, had a certain amount of risk attached. "It sounds like fascism."

Su translated. To my surprised relief they all nodded and with great confirming energy, and Jin said at once, "Yes, fascism, but"—he raised a cautionary finger—"it was fascism with feudalism and that is far worse."

"Can you talk about it? I believe what you tell me but I am still not sure I understand their motivation. I mean, it sounds as if they simply did not want movies or plays or books to exist. What would they reply to that?"

Jin laughed and they all joined in; I had apparently struck a nerve. He sighed and launched into his explanation. "Do you know about the Three Prominences?"

"Vaguely, I think I've read somewhere that—"

He broke in. "Jiang Qing's aesthetic—which, you understand, was rigidly enforced in all art forms—required that there be Three

Prominences in any revolutionary work. There had to be a Bad Element, who is actually a spy or agent of imperialism, a group of worker-peasant heroes or Number Two Heroes, and finally a Number One Hero, or Hero of the Heroes. The Number One Hero, of course, can have no inner conflicts, no personal weaknesses, and naturally no character.*

"In fact, the Number Two Heroes were cast whenever possible from actors of the same height. Incidentally, to enroll in any acting school or theater company your family had to be workers or peasants for at least three generations. By the end of their reign, needless to say, there were more teachers than students."

Another man interrupted. "We now have more than ten thousand applicants for film schools and two thousand in the Drama School in Peking."

I asked Jin Shan, "And what about the audiences? Did they like the plays with the Three Prominences?"

Jin Shan

"Oh, there are always some who enjoy that kind of arithmetic." Jin Shan grinned. "But you will see mostly young people in our theaters now, and I can assure you very few came voluntarily to see the Three Prominences. But the problem is not over; many younger writers' minds are still captured by this formula and some of them honestly don't know how to struggle out of it. That is why we have so few good scenarists. The people who grew up in the past ten years are not yet capable of dealing with life. I suppose you know about the Eight Model Works?"

They all smiled, partly embarrassed but mainly in relief at being able to joke about it. Said Jin Shan, "The Empress finally decided that China needed no more than eight plays."

"You're kidding."

"This unfortunately is the truth. Not only was eight the limit, but their real authors' names were in some cases omitted or accompanied by the names of committees who they claimed had written them. And all without exception were advertised as having been 'inspired by Jiang Qing,' who really took the authorial credit."

"In other words," I said, "the idea was to keep any individual from standing out."

"Except for herself, yes. Herself and the other three."

The actress added, "She made films lauding herself. *Counterattack* praises her wildly . . ."

A director said, "*Grand Festival* praised them all, but it never got finished."

Jin Shan asked, "You knew nothing about this?"

"Very little. It's hard to say why. I think I read more than most people about China, but somehow the impact of it all never hit me.

* "Persist in the principle of creating characters in which the best and highest of the working class is portrayed, *unrestricted by real life and people*." *China Reconstructs*, August 1976.

Frankly, it's all still so moronic it's hard to take in . . ."

Again they laughed, nodding to one another, and the actress, confirming my remark, added, "They made a film, *Daughter of the Slave*, about a slave of the Yi people, and to be sure that you could tell who the heroine was they dressed her in a pink blouse. It was like pointing at her with an arrow."

I could not disbelieve them, but neither could I grasp the evolution of their disaster, and groping for something in common with these fellow professionals, I asked if they taught any special theory of acting, such as Stanislavsky's.

"Stani," as his name is said here, is indeed the basic theorist, but they seemed a bit uneasy at saying so, and added that they had their own Chinese version, which was not quite pure. (The five plays I would soon see had no trace of his influence, the operatic influence overwhelming the realism.)

"What about the future," I asked, "or is it too soon to talk about that?"

"Well, for example," Jin said, "they chased away the entire staff of the Shanghai Film Studio, the best we had in China. Work was suspended there for nine years. But we're starting slowly to put things back together again."

I decided to ask this group about names I had been given the day before of film people who had met particularly gruesome ends. "Did you know Xian Bai Mo?"

"He was a scenarist," one of the men said. "He was beaten to death. He was very open in his opposition to the Lady."

"And Zheng Chunli?"

"He was a director of films. In fact, one of his films is showing in America now. He was tortured to death but it is not known precisely why."

Rewi Alley, an eighty-year-old New Zealander who had spent half a century in China, had told me of these names and fates the previous evening. He had also said that Lao She, author of *Rickshaw Boy*, a great hit in America thirty-five years ago, had been killed at the age of seventy. (Some say that he committed suicide in despair and as an anti-Mao protest.)

We had been talking for about an hour now and I needed a couple of minutes to reorganize; for I realized that without planning to I had come to China, a one-party state, poorly prepared by time spent in the Soviet Union, Czechoslovakia, Poland, and Hungary. Of course these people too were hewing to a line—the villainies of the Gang of Four. But I had been in the Soviet Union in the mid-sixties during the "de-Stalinization" time, and Russians even then did not half so openly and self-assuredly tell of sufferings the dictator had caused. His very name was still uneasily spoken and not without a certain psychological glance over the shoulder, quite as though he might rise from his grave. They knew, in Russia, that Stalinists still controlled the big jobs and no doubt the police. And in China too the adherents of the Four had by no means been cleaned out of public life. Was this outspoken interview with me part of the struggle to prevent their enemies from regrouping? I thought so. Rewi Alley had said that many Four supporters had been expelled from their jobs and given lesser ones, and he had quoted Mao on how to deal with people whose ideas are wrong: "People are not chives; their heads do not grow back when they are cut off." This interview, then, was part of the ongoing battle.

But I knew I had still not understood the terms of that battle. To Zheng Zenyao, the weeping pupil of the murdered actress, I tried to explain myself. "I apologize for my stupidity but for some reason I have never been aware of the extent of your sufferings. But I still am not clear why a woman like, for instance, your dear friend Sun Weishi, was so targeted. Is there some specific reason?"

Jin Shan took over now, and his smile was gone. "My wife, aside from her great popularity as an actress—which you understand now was a challenge to our Empress—was also very close to Zhou Enlai. This was very well known. My wife's parents had been martyred by the Guo Mindang, and she was alone in the world and in effect was adopted by Zhou. He also saw to it that she was trained as an actress. So that by the time our Empress had gathered power, my wife was Director of the Experimental Theater. She introduced Ostrovsky, Goldoni, Chekhov, Gogol . . ."

"When would this be?"

"The fifties and early sixties. But her reputation as an actress was very great even before the Liberation in 1949. Her fate was a direct attack on Premier Zhou. Madame Mao made a special point of having my wife's head shaved in detention."

I was still unsatisfied. "I guess what I am asking is, why this intense hostility to Zhou?"

Jin Shan grinned. "Yes. There are political reasons, but you know, of course, that he opposed her wedding."

"To Chairman Mao?"

"She never forgave him for that. And of course my wife refused to do what they asked her to."

"And what was that?"

"To condemn Premier Zhou and his line."

"How? Could you give me an example?"

They all laughed at both my ignorance and my persistence. One man said, "It would hardly matter—Jiang Qing had to destroy Zhou's influence on the country in any way she could. One time he stated his admiration for Beethoven, for example. She proceeded at once to expound a new line against playing Beethoven or any European music and actually forbade it and it was no longer played."

I remembered reading about their forbidding Beethoven and my thinking that the Chinese indeed were inscrutable. So it was all petty and bitchy! Suddenly it seemed to have lost all political meaning, even if it was filled with political consequence. A personal power fight, that was all.

But the pressing thought now was what Mao must have been like to have remained connected to this trivial woman. I dared not venture that question and feigned naïveté instead. "And how did it appear at the time?—all this absurdity? Not that we Americans haven't had our own, but I am trying to share your feelings now; do you think of yourselves as being dupes, or what?"

I knew perfectly well how embarrassing such ex post facto questions always are—how could we have twice given Nixon his unprecedented pluralities?

Jin Shan seemed slightly to resent the question, while at the same time recognizing its validity. "If Othello had known in time what Iago was, there would not have been a tragedy. The Cultural Revolution began as a good and necessary thing; any movement can be perverted. But the earth continues to turn and history goes forward. And so we have confidence."

As comprehensible, if not predictable, as his answer was, it left a sense of hopelessness that an outsider could ever find in Western experience any useful analogues to what these people had been through, and where it had left them politically and spiritually. No one could doubt their sincerity in condemning Jiang Qing and the Four, but it was still for the moment impossible to include Chairman Mao's part in the common disaster. I had entered into the unacknowledged etiquette without being aware of it; I too chose not to lay any emphasis on the perfectly apparent fact that many of the people in the room had been in trouble well before the Gang had taken all power in hand, before Mao had become—if indeed he had become—incompetent to control the state.

I had more to ask but people now were rising to depart. Jin Shan, however, kept his seat and thus prevented them from dispersing, and he called to me over the patter of talk that had broken out, "What about Hollywood?—is it still making movies?"

I explained that the great studios had disintegrated with the coming of television, news they seemed surprised and rather disappointed to hear, but that the much admired Hollywood technical equipment had not been liquidated was reassuring, evidently.

"And Charles Laughton? What does he do now?" Jin Shan wanted to know.

I said that Laughton had died years ago and the room quieted in deference, I thought, as well as surprise.

Another director asked what Clark Gable was doing. Another asked about William Powell, the actress asked after Joan Crawford, and Edward G. Robinson was asked after, and the Marx Brothers, and there were other names too, and all of them were dead. I could

Tien An Men Square, Peking

hardly ask them what they felt about this, how it felt to land on the earth from somewhere in space after an absence of years, many years, in fact. But from their muted looks, and a certain inwardness that my funerary news had given their expressions, I thought they must also be sorting out their feelings on returning to the world.

It was the wrong time to ask the question but we were clearly breaking up and I did want their reaction. "Is any thought being given to preventing all this happening again?"

There was silence and I instantly regretted the question because, quite obviously, they could not be expected to know the answer, which would be in the hands of political people, if indeed it was a live question at all. Still, they did not seem to think it altogether foolish of me to have asked, and Jin Shan, as he was being helped to his feet by the actress, looked me fully in the eyes and smiled and said, "That of course is the question," at which they all nodded and murmured and agreed, and they seemed to feel him a bit brave to have said this to me.

"Are you able to work again?" I asked him.

Once more, as I realized when heads turned in surprise, I had verged on a gaffe, and from the grin on his face it was clear that Jin required a moment to forgive me.

It was like having asked Cecil B. De Mille if he was doing anything these days as he stepped off the set of *The Ten Commandments*. "I have been shooting in Daqing for almost two years now," he said, and I knew at once he was indeed involved in an epic. Daqing is an oil field discovered in 1964 and exploited solely by Chinese without Soviet or other outside help, and symbolizes the power of ordinary untrained people to create technological wonders without enslavement by "experts." It was perhaps the most substantial demonstration of the Cultural Revolution's basic thesis of proletarian self-reliance.

And obviously, in the context of this gathering of victims of the Cultural Revolution, or at least of its excesses, I was at a loss to understand how Jin had chosen this subject when he had hardly recovered from detention by Cultural Revolutionaries. But every question has three sides in China and his explanation proceeded: "The film is not about the Iron Man of Daqing . . ."

"Incidentally," I interrupted, "is the Iron Man a real person?"

"Oh, yes. But you must know what they did to him."

The Iron Man was a fabulous hero whose example of prowess, ingenuity, bravery, and physical endurance had fired the people to persist in the work of the Daqing complex. He was the real-life hero, apparently, whom Jiang Qing's Three Prominences were attempting to fabricate on the stage.

Jin Shan continued, "They sent gangsters to torture him, you know."

"The Four?"

"They suspended him by wires tied to his toes and fingers, and then laid bricks on his body."

"What was the point?" I asked. Again it was the campaign to bring down Zhou Enlai. The Iron Man must confess "that the red banner of Daqing was a black banner in fact . . ."

In short, in this highly symbolic culture a famed hero was to slander Zhou and thus turn people against him. "They tied buckets to his neck by fine wires, and gradually filled them up with water. They forced his head into a heated box in a wall and, when he fainted, revived him and repeated it. But he refused to reverse his allegiance to Zhou.

"But Song Sunming, who is our oil industry minister"—Jin laughed—"they called him the 'King of Oil'—was also tortured in Daqing and he couldn't stand it and issued the statement they wanted, but he later recanted. But my film, *The Rising Sun*, is actually about the women of Daqing. It's based on a play which my late wife starred in before her arrest and which was especially praised by Zhou. Mao said that 'women support half the sky,' but the men of Daqing, as elsewhere in China, are not always ready to accord them their place. To be honest"—Jin smiled—"I am not sure yet that I have overcome my own male contradictions. But I am trying. Anyway, the plot of the film is more terrible than *Macbeth* . . ."

Now he extended his hand to Inge and me. "Enjoy your travels. Stay longer next time." And with his late wife's pupil hovering close by him, he turned and left, trailed by the others.

I knew that he despaired of ever being able to explain what he was feeling now, what he remembered, or even what he hoped would come to pass. Who has not had the experience of attempting to explain to foreigners the tangled and paradoxical nuances of a decade or two gone by? But here it was even more desperately difficult, for they were the victims of a movement, the Great Cultural Revolution, for whose moral and even political aims they had profound respect if not awe, and whose perversions—as they saw it—had robbed them of great chunks of their lives.

If I did not have the key to their sense of life now it did seem, nevertheless, that I had stumbled on one great question their sufferings had left them with—how to prevent their disaster from repeating itself. For there was no doubt at all that fundamentally nothing in the structure of the system had really been changed by their travail.

[3]

"The visitor who stays a month writes a book, the one who stays three months does an article, and those who move in for years never write anything." Frank Coe, sipping his beer and chain-smoking his cigarettes, was sitting in the overgrown garden of his Peking house on one of the new wicker chairs his wife had recently bought. In the fifties he had been an associate of the U.S. Treasury official Harry Dexter White, and accused like White of something like treasonous loyalties to the Red Chinese. Finding himself unemployable in the States, Coe had accepted a job with the then brand-new Mao government as an adviser on economics.

His wife, Ruth, works at editing the English-language bulletin published daily in Peking for foreigners. It is one of China's surprises: a sheaf of clips from the Western as well as Chinese news agencies, many of them not at all pro-Red and some directly contradicting the official line. The Chinese-language edition, small by their standards, is now run off in 16,000,000 copies and circulates widely. An equivalent surprise might be the U.S. government circulating every morning at its own expense Tass and Xinhua news stories.

The young Coe daughter speaks better Chinese than English, but Coe speaks no Chinese. His elegant house, in the old upper-class Peking style, is set within a spacious closed courtyard but is far more elaborate than most, having belonged to a long-gone capitalist. Many works of Chinese art are hung, removed, and rehung on the fragile-looking filigreed walls. The Coes are restless. Ruth has come back to the States several times in recent years and, so it seems, would not mind returning home for good. Coe, however, is an exile. And from China too, perhaps. He speaks without bitterness of the past, but the bitterness is there as it must be; he seems, as he sits in the weedy garden surrounded by its brick wall, like a being encased in an endless afternoon, something motionless and remote in the air around him. He coughs, smokes, smiles, and coughs again. He is one of that tiny tribe of Americans who perceived too soon that America and the Chinese Revolution were not and need not try to be enemies to the death.* It is not with unmixed gratification that he now sees both countries drawing closer at last. It could have happened a quarter of a century ago and spared America her Korean and Vietnamese casualties, for one thing. For another, it would have spared Frank Coe and the others their lives of perpetual estrangement and exile.

But, as with the others, his Maoist perspective permits no such regrets, and he knows that somewhere in the ligatures of history the useless conflict was determined and necessary. Far more than he or they were wasted in the past quarter century. A reputable economist and for a time professor at the University of Toronto, he wrote a paper from Peking in the fifties based on figures given him by government people, figures that had been boiled, as the jargon

Frank Coe, Peking

* Premier Zhou Enlai tried in 1945 to get U.S. Embassy permission to fly to Washington and explain the Chinese Revolution to President Roosevelt. Permission was refused.

has it, so that he found himself having purveyed something like falsehood. He persisted in understanding the government's misuse of him—more was at stake than Frank Coe's academic reputation, which the revolution was not obliged to respect. But, nevertheless, it made his return to the States impossible, in his estimate. Observing him now—a man in his seventies, rather dapper in dress, newly shaved in the afternoon when, as usual, he greets his day—one cannot help resenting his misuse, forgetting momentarily that power everywhere has always been the deadliest game of all. Is, was, and will be, and nothing is so futile as lamenting it or the ever-lasting mutual attraction of power and untruth. Perhaps a Coe is wiser to take some pleasure in the usefully possible—he shows a certain modest contentment in producing a handsome, newly printed volume of Mao's *Works* in English, which he spent a year polishing. I note as I flip the pages in the dusty sunlight of the silent garden that no translator's or English editor's name appears anywhere in the book and say so, and he coughs and smiles without commenting—the books of the very great spring from the head of Jove, as we all know, and human intercession is distracting to think about.

Sol Adler, on the other hand, seems less an exile than a perky voyager to another land, even though he has also spent nearly half his life in China. Inge and I are charmed by his and Mrs. Adler's house, also surrounded by a protective garden wall, but newly done over in white and red high-gloss paint, with all sorts of rooms opening off a garden, and a young, white-jacketed Chinese cook and general factotum who lives beside the great entrance gate. Adler does not know who owns the house and seems hardly concerned to find out. He is English by birth, but also worked in the U.S. Treasury when the roof fell in during the Truman time and charges of treason flew around Washington like summer lightning.

Adler is in pain tonight, and is due for a hospital stay tomorrow for an examination of what he fears is a stomach ulcer. He is tense, unable to sit still, skinny and tall and grimacing with anguish, but insists on accompanying us at dinner. I had wanted to speak to him for the facts he might have about the economy, and he delights in making clear differentiations.

"Of course everyone wants to believe that under the Gang the economy went completely to pot, but I've got the figures finally—just got them this week—and here's the picture. There was practically no change in production for '74 and '75. It just all hung there. But the '76 and '77 figures show the slide. It was beginning to collapse and you could well talk about an approaching bankruptcy, in effect. The graph began a real tilt just then."

"What were they after, can you tell?"

"Well, there's no question they wanted to pull up the gangplank and go back to the traditional isolation of China. Example—they changed over the Shanghai electrical turbines from coal to oil so as to cut down the amount of oil they could possibly sell to Japan. It was absolutely loony. But it's a deep strain in the Chinese character, this idea that they don't need the rest of the world."

"Like the U.S."

"Well, yes, in the old days. The isolationists. You know, of course, I suppose, that you'd have found it perfectly useless to try to talk to Chinese a couple of years ago, they'd have been too suspicious— in fact they'd have been scared to death of you."

I repeated the question preying on my mind. "Frank Coe," I said, "seems to feel that there could be a repetition of the Four, another sort of seizure of power by a determined faction of the Central Committee."

"Of course, yes. That sort of thing could happen again."

"But nobody seems terribly exercised about it," I said. "Coe feels that it's the Party's duty to speak up about mistakes it sees, and to insist on the state not having the right to retaliate against critics, but . . ."

"That's not always so easy to prevent," Adler admitted.

"Exactly. Coe said the same. But I gather it isn't on the front burner even, despite what's happened. I mean, specifically some institutional change that will make it perfectly legal and safe for a minority critical voice to be heard before the country goes smash following the majority line."

"Yes, I know," he said, nodding and thinking. But I suspected that he also knew that behind my feeling was an as yet inadmissible challenge to the Party's monopoly of power and thought. I said as much. It was pleasant talking to Adler—his British tolerance, despite his evident stomach pain, made conversation easy. But it inevitably flitted across my mind that neither he nor the other "revolutionary pensioners" had dared criticize the burgeoning calamity while they were witnessing it.

"The problem is not simply the Party's monopoly of thought, of course. This country moved directly from semi-feudalism into socialism, without the interval of capitalism . . ."

"Coe said that too . . ."

"Yes, it's quite obvious but important anyway. They never had a tradition of Western-type individualism. I mean in particular the notion that any individual was invested with a sort of existence entirely to one side of society. Although Mao, you know, expected there to be a period of capitalism after the revolution."

"He actually saw it as a revolution against feudalism?"

"I think there's no question of that. And a sort of infantile period of Chinese capitalism did last about four years, but it never

Sol Adler, Peking

gathered any strength and simply fell like a soufflé. In four years the state owned everything, you see."

For Mrs. Adler, an Englishwoman and a former schoolteacher, who had come to China "to see," and then remained to teach English, the repeated entrances of their linen-jacketed young cook with yet another course of our dinner was overwhelming; he was new with them and in this refurbished house completed an uncustomarily luxurious atmosphere. The room was sparsely furnished in the Chinese manner, a few very fine pieces set within broad empty spaces, and one or two scroll paintings on wide expanses of white wall. Mrs. Adler worked hard teaching all day, had found in China her cause and her reason for living. A happy and devoted woman dressed in blouse and an unmatching skirt. But clothes could not matter, obviously.

"Coe said that Jiang Qing actually tried to get control of Mao's book royalties, is that what you heard?" I asked.

"Oh, that's known. In fact, the royalties were all the money he had. He only made four hundred and fifty yuan a month. But let's talk about something else. If you are going to write about this place, don't say that they are 'all Chinese.' This is a common misconception. There's a babble of dialects that are incomprehensible from one district to another, as though the Welsh still couldn't manage English, you know. And they're racially quite differentiated and look different to one another even if they're all alike to outsiders. And you mustn't think they're inept—China exports machinery to the Third World, you know . . ."

His delivery was fast and helter-skelter and one could see the surges of pain as he spoke. "And about Harry Dexter White. He was really the author—not Keynes—of the International Monetary Fund. Keynes vastly admired White, you know, and himself was quite candid about White's authorship. He dropped dead of heart failure . . ."

"The Un-American Activities Committee . . ."

"Well, his attack happened to come when they were hounding him, yes, but White really died of work, intensely hard work for the United States government. That's the important thing, you know." Like Coe, Adler had been under White's wing in the Treasury Department in those long-dead days. Now he advises the Chinese on Western economies and his life seems filled with work. The fall of the Gang for him was the opening of a welcome new era when China would face out to the world.

"We've been to the bookstores," I said. "There are long lines of mostly young people stretching out into the streets. They're advertising on slates outside that they've got *Robinson Crusoe, Tom Sawyer*, and something by Balzac . . ."

"Yes, it's very exciting. They've been starved for any foreign literature."

Line at bookstore, Peking

"It's interesting that even though they were cut off for so long they really do want to know foreign stuff . . ."

"It's a whole generation, you see," he said, "that's had no education at all, as far as that goes."

"The whole thing is stupefying, isn't it?" I said. "I mean the idea of isolating the largest country in the world like this . . . it's hard to conceive." He nodded silently. "Could you pinpoint the date when Jiang Qing took over? When would you say Mao had lost command?"

Adler, controlling his grimace of pain, thought about this for a moment. And I knew as I watched him that he shared the vague sense of disorientation that every Chinese had evinced when I had asked that question. "Actually, that's very difficult to say exactly . . ."

As he paused again to stare and think, I felt the same sensation as when I had asked it of the Chinese—the conversation and we ourselves seemed to become enfolded in some immense banner of rippling gray silk. I was aware by this time, of course, that Mao may well have been in agreement with the now-hated Four. Or perhaps, as some suggested, his Parkinson's disease had kept him out of touch. Then again, maybe it hadn't, and what was now called fascism could not easily be separated from him. Thus this suspension of the past in a timeless and impervious cell, this blurring of the shape of events gone by which left the past like a plasmic lump without beginning or end and a crazy old actress sitting on top of it all, yelling her ignorant commands and endlessly writing her own name. That spectacle, I thought, must be terrible to contemplate for Marxists, whose pride is to have left irrationality to capitalism.

"You have to remember," he said, "that initially the Cultural Revolution—"

"What date are we talking about?" I asked, resolving once and for all to penetrate the morass.

"Well, around '66. Mao, you know, was really trying to create a kind of Renaissance person who could do a little of everything. The object was political, naturally—to prevent a hardening of the elite, to keep the Party's nose in the armpit of the people. The scientist should be able to swing a pickax, the peasant should have an equal say in construction plans. But the spirit of this kind of thing is absolutely essential to keep pure, and the Gang distorted it terribly. Mao was not, for instance, a leveler. He had no interest in taking vengeance on someone just because that person was gifted or intelligent. But the Gang simply swept whole classes of students out of school and put them to feeding pigs."

"I had the impression they volunteered for farm work . . ."

"Some certainly did."

"But most were dragooned."

"Well . . . they were, yes."

"Was Mao against that?"

He knew no more than anyone else how to answer. And I wondered whether this amnesia-like affect was also due to the common human inability to recall a lost enthusiasm. Nothing is more inexplicable than a vanished zeal. It's like a love affair gone sour—how could one have been ready to kill or die for her or him?

And deeper down in the belly, of course, must lie puzzlement that the redeemer Mao, and the revolution itself, could have borne a fatal flaw into the world. Here, indeed, was the ultimate space that Adler and China herself could not, at least not yet, dare examine critically. It was understandable. Too much that was evil had been swept away by the revolution and too many good and honest people had died to give it its victory. And so it would probably be a while yet before one could know more or less precisely when the Great Cultural Revolution had gone bad.

[4]

As guests of the Association for Friendship with Foreign Countries we travel alone, not in a group, but with our hard-working guide-interpreter Su Guang usually by our side. To lighten long train rides and those inevitable longueurs during interminable auto tours on bad roads, I can kid Su about his naps. He is a civilized man of thirty-two and expects any human who can possibly do so to drop off for a few minutes after lunch. It is my opinion that either he cuts out the naps or the Four Modernizations—of agriculture, industry, science and technology, and defense—will be delayed by at least another generation. It takes Su a couple of days to interpret my signals, and with Inge's help he is finally reassured that I am not being serious, and by the second week of our time together he is even cracking a few mildly satirical jokes of his own at my expense.

It is worth pointing out that we don't believe Su Guang is a secret policeman. For one thing, Inge can and does get the car to stop unexpectedly anywhere along the streets and roads where she sees something to photograph, some of it not at all flattering to a country eager to show its best face or to conceal its worst.

Thrown together with Su for twelve hours a day, we find life becoming less and less formal among us. To some degree, one inevitably sees the country through his eyes and China gradually becomes less dramatic, less incongruous, a bit more repetitive and consequently a little more real. Whatever failings the Chinese character has, boasting is not one of them, and in 1978 neither is that time-honored and ludicrous mendaciousness of government guides whenever a perfectly evident failing of their system arises. For

Left to right: Su Guang, Qiao Yu, Arthur Miller

example, it is we who are enthusiastic about the hundreds of people we see everywhere, in courtyards and on the streets before public buildings where they are about to enter work, exercising with the Tai Ji method. Whole troops of office workers can be seen on sidewalks staring into space as they visualize clouds and vapors which, with slow and gracefully tensed hands, they attempt to shape and move from place to place, at the same time bending the trunk and legs and turning, twisting, and stretching. But Su Guang is not an exerciser, and regardless of the credit it may give his country, he would rather remain seated if at all possible.

It is I who note that bicycles seem to be parked almost anywhere without chains and padlocks, while Su is sorry to have to tell me that they are in fact locked across the rear wheel by a discreet built-in device because they are not infrequently stolen. Moreover, near markets or other gathering places, there are old ladies who keep watch on parked bikes for a small tip. If there is nothing like the volume of thievery that exists in New York no opportunity is lost to hang a padlock where it will do the most good.

And it is Su Guang who informs us, after I have noted how clean the people seem, "Well, some of them are not so clean. But it is hard to keep clean."

"No hot water?"

"No bathtubs."

Tai Ji Quan: morning exercises, Peking

This piece of news slightly alters the picturesqueness of the cold-water tap one usually sees in Peking courtyards, especially when one thinks of January and February . . .

Over the days it becomes clear that if he has not been formally ordered to speak the truth, he nevertheless understands it is his duty even at times when it is a bit painful to do so. One must inevitably read into his honesty a political footnote of sorts, for if he had been instructed to conceal or deny certain evidences of their backwardness, he would have no choice but to obey. And it is he, not I, who uses the word "backward."

The result of his candor is that, with such as he, one sets aside the well-known tendency to shout psychologically, so to speak, at one another for lack of the means to express nuances. It is dishonesty that creates our barriers far more than cultural differences or even language; it is the defensiveness of political systems trying to feign success, not only to foreigners, but fundamentally to themselves.

Nevertheless, our observations clash as we look, for example, at the street crowds among which there seem to be extraordinarily few couples simply walking along together—not to speak of men and women touching or holding hands. I thought Su would surely agree that there were very few.

Not only does he disagree, but so does my wife, who thinks there is the usual number of couples. I still believe that among the Chinese there are far more men and women who leave a spouse home when they go out, even with their small children. It is perfectly common to see a man going along with an infant on his hip, holding it over the curb to relieve itself through the slit in the pants—they don't use diapers—but rare to see a couple with children.

Su's own parents are dead—his mother died only last year, of cancer, and just when he was guiding a group of American cancer specialists on a tour. His family were peasants and he is the only one of five or six children who went to higher schools. In the midst of one crowd near the Sun Yat-sen Memorial in Nanjing on National Day, their Fourth of July, I wondered if any peasants had come into town to celebrate.

"There are peasants all around us right now," he said.

I looked at the dozens of people who were clustering around Inge, fascinated by her many slung cameras. They were all dressed precisely the same, of course, in the Sun Yat-sen jacket misnamed the Mao jacket abroad. "How can you tell?" I asked.

"The ones with dark skins. Like mine."

"You mean it's genetic?"

"I guess so—I'm not in the sun very much, but I'm still dark."

We are at the foot of the thousand-step stairway which flows down from the Sun Yat-sen Memorial and now Su learns, with what can only be described as excruciating happiness, that I intend to sit down with him and novelist Ai Xuan and let Inge and a local woman interpreter ascend by themselves. (In each city protocol requires a local interpreter to accompany, regardless of Su's presence.)

But all the stone benches bordering the stairway are wholly or partly occupied, and as I look about for a place and suggest we sit on a step, Ai Xuan approaches three people seated on a bench and says, "Make room, please, for this foreign friend of China," with which the three, two young men and a middle-aged woman with her five-year-old child in hand, instantly stand up and nod happily to me, as though it is I who am doing the favor, and, gesturing for me to sit down, walk off into the dense crowd which ceaselessly descends from the memorial above.

The charm of this performance is disturbed by an uneasy sense of its unreality, to say nothing of its unfairness. It attaches itself to a string of earlier incidents which jangle together in the mind. For one, Su is not allowed to eat with us, his charges, but joins his fellow Chinese in a separate hotel dining room unless his presence as interpreter is required. And while he never complains, his food is not really as good or as varied and interesting as ours.

There is also the question of the army guard whom one sometimes—although not always—sees at the bottom of a hotel driveway, his rifle at port arms, bayonet fixed. Usually a very young soldier, he crisply salutes all incoming cars, and in response to my asking what the man is guarding, Su shrugs and is at a loss. "Probably a leftover from the past," he says, dismissing it.

But back home after our China trip, we meet a young San Francisco-born Chinese girl whose cousin had had a curious experience with such a guard. The cousin had bought herself a standard Sun Yat-sen jacket and trousers, a "set," as it is called, and after trying it on in her hotel had tied her hair in pigtails just as so many Chinese girls do, and had gone out of the hotel. When, later, she returned and started up the front steps, a guard suddenly appeared, pushed her away, and when she protested, called her some untidy names and asked who the hell she thought she was coming off the street into a fine hotel like this. Unfortunately, she had left her U.S. passport in her room and it took some time to get herself identified as an overseas Chinese, after which the guard nervously apologized. If foreigners are free to photograph and move about, not quite at random but with relative freedom, there is evidently still some distance to travel before the bars go all the way down for the right of Chinese to do the same. By all accounts, however, it is only in the past year or so that even foreigners were allowed so long a leash, so perhaps the improvement can be expected to continue until it reaches the natives.

One unexpected proof of this recently altered state of affairs occurred on our first morning in China, when we decided to go for a walk through Peking back streets alone, before Su Guang appeared to pick us up after breakfast. At about seven-thirty that fine autumn morning we left the hotel and simply turned corners at random. At this early stage of our trip the poverty of the houses struck me powerfully; except for the brick instead of adobe construction one might be in a backwater Mexican town. Yet the vigor of the people was as undeniable as the absence of the least timidity or fear in their stares at us. The smell of burning carbon in the air from their cookstoves, the ever-present dust in the streets, the low-lying and often beautifully shaped boat-like roofs, mixed an air of serenity with the decrepitude of the structures. But there was no smell of decay in the air, or of sewage or the usual fetid stenches of poverty, and this freshness of the atmosphere, along with the trim cleanliness of the people, was at odds with the visual evidence of crowding. There was no sense of civic demoralization if the eye and nose can judge such things.

Suddenly, out of a narrow alleyway a man appeared pushing his bicycle; he was old, surely in his mid-seventies, with stringy white whiskers and, unusually enough, his tunic collar carelessly unbuttoned. He looked as if he had just jumped out of bed and was late, but seeing us, he halted at the opening of his little alley and seemed about to fly apart in astonishment. His lips began to tremble and his eyes teared.

Inge began to offer him a Chinese "good morning"—her first

First encounter, Peking

really public attempt to use the language she had studied for four years and could now read and write on a high level indeed, but before she could speak he asked—in halting but reasonable English!—who we were, where we were from, and what we were doing here of all places, slowly gathering his wits under a barrage of feelings that were all variations of delight.

"Imagine!" he called out breathlessly, "finding you people here, right out on the *street*! And being able to speak to you like this!"

We were still so new in China that his astonishment was hard to understand.

"But even a year ago I wouldn't have dared come up to you like this—even if they'd let you go around alone . . . no, no, not the police, the neighbors would have had me in all kinds of trouble." And he glanced around challengingly at the huddle of houses on his little street as though hoping one of the neighbors would see him out here talking to us legally. "We've been hounded for years, you see . . . this awful fear and hatred of foreigners. I couldn't possibly have even approached you, and now"—he beamed—"here we are! And we can talk about anything at all!"

He had studied English in Japan in the thirties, like not a few Chinese of that time, and was so eager to see us again that we made a date with him to meet in our hotel that evening. And we found him when we returned at the end of the day, sitting erectly in one of the overstuffed chairs on our floor and looking at us reproachfully as we walked over to him. "You are late," he said, quite abruptly. In fact, we had forgotten all about him and apologized for the half hour we had made him wait. He relented, but only slowly, and got down to business, offering to act as our guide through China. He could drop everything and begin tomorrow morning.

What was surprising was not his eye for business or adventure or both, but that he could live only a couple of blocks away from one of the biggest tourist hotels where foreigners by the hundreds came and went constantly, always accompanied by Chinese guides, and yet have no awareness that this shepherding system prevailed and that we could not improvise some private arrangement with him. Once again, as trivial as this instance might be, a certain imponderable sense arose from it of an individual isolation, something cut off and remote in each person—in this case an alert and intelligent old man. We invited him to come again the following evening but he never showed up.

But to return to our newly won seat beside the vast stairs leading up to Sun Yat-sen's Memorial—the three of us men gratefully relaxed on the bench and waved goodbye to Inge and the local interpreter, as they melted into the crowd climbing upward toward the sky-blue roof of the seemingly mile-high memorial building.

With the temperature so perfect, in the mid-seventies, and a light breeze blowing, I found myself regretting the unisex drabness of their women's unvarying trousers-tunic set on this, their chief day of celebration.

"Su, old buddy," I said, "one of these days in between naps you ought to get the word to the higher-ups that a lot of these people are girls."

He was on to me by this time and pretended to be outraged. "Of course, they are girls. We know that."

"How about letting them wear skirts sometimes?"

"It's not the season."

"But it's a warm day."

"Yes, but it's October."

"No skirts after September?"

"Not usually, no. It's just a fashion."

"Well, I won't argue. But it's very discouraging."

Su translated for Ai Xuan, who, behind his lenses, blinked with amusement and said, "Perhaps that will change now, too, like other things. She . . ." (by this time Jiang Qing was merely referred to in the third person, so frequent was the mention of her in contexts like this) "enforced a strong puritanical fashion on the people. Although privately, of course, her life was quite different."

"Boyfriends?"

His own personal modesty seemed to forbid him more than a circumlocution. "All kinds of behavior. You know, she was having elaborate gowns made in the style of an empress."

"Do you really think she was serious about being an empress?" I asked as skeptically as possible.

"Worse than an empress," Su quickly put in, "a female emperor!"

"Ai Xuan," I said, "why don't I ever see a man and woman touching? It is a very rare sight, you know."

Su again intervened. I knew by now that he was genuinely mystified by any persistent curiosity about their sexual mores. But it was less mere embarrassment on his part than bewilderment at the general importance such personal matters could possibly have. "It is not our tradition," he said with some protest, "we just don't do that in public."

I turned to Ai Xuan; he was five years older than Su Guang, a direct fellow and quick to laugh. He too had done time under restraint out in the country, but the experience had apparently not depressed him, unlike almost everyone else. "I like peasants. Most of my friends now are peasants," he said.

"The Cultural Revolution didn't hurt them?"

"Not very much. For them it was something that was going on in the cities. And very few of them took any active part in all that. There was no big connection they could see between the Cultural Revolution and their income and the work, which doesn't change

Left to right: Arthur Miller, Ai Xuan, Su Guang at the Sun Yat-sen mausoleum, Nanjing

much." He had an open, uncomplicated spirit and was probably closer to being a majority man than others we would meet.

"You think the Cultural Revolution did much damage?"

"Well, yes, but it's all remedied now. We can't always move straight ahead; the truth goes like a river, no river is straight."

"You don't feel, then, that your detainment lost you a lot of time?"

"Yes, but who knows if I wouldn't have lost time for some other reason . . .?"

Out of nowhere a young couple popped up before us and posed together while a friend snapped their picture. The young man had his arm slung over his girlfriend's shoulders. I turned to Su Guang. "I was wrong, they do make contact."

Su Guang for some reason did not look happy with his victory.

"What's wrong now?"

"They were not Chinese, for one thing," Su said.

"What then?"

"They were Malaysian."

"But even so you don't approve?"

"I don't approve . . . yet." And he smiled at his conflict. "It is really against our tradition."

"You mean, they either actually make love, or nothing?"

"No. Later on, when it gets dark, people can . . ." he laughed, embarrassed, "have heart-to-heart talks."

We sat silent for a moment watching the crowd. Then I said, "You know why it's important?"

"No, I don't," said Su.

"Because it's all about to change, and so fast your heads will spin."

"We know that. It changes already," Su said.

"Like what?"

"Girl babies are as good as boy babies." His good citizen's pride did not entirely conceal his own uneasiness, however. "They have to be equal; we cannot have so many children."

"You mean, people keep trying for a boy."

"That's the problem—the in-laws force these population increases, by requiring a boy to please the ancestors. But they will have to be pleased by a girl now."

"Your child is a boy, though."

"Oh, yes. Spring Thunder is his name," and he couldn't help the satisfaction that floated into his eyes at the mention of his son.

"So you don't have to take another shot at it."

"No, no, we shall have only one."

"What are the advantages of having a boy? Women work now, earn the same, don't they?"

"Boys stay home to support their parents in old age. Girls go off with their husbands."

Ai Xuan

"You will have a happy old age, then."

"I am not thinking of my old age!" He laughed in protest. "Why are you always thinking about the future?"

For no reason, the question came to my tongue now. "Ai Xuan, may I ask you if there are any writers in prison in China?"

The novelist's eyes opened wider in surprise. "Now?"

"Yes."

"Oh, no, no, not now. But before, of course."

"How long were you actually held?"

"For three years. They had me in the pig sties."

We stared at the mass of people climbing and descending, most of them young and many of them looking directly at me as they passed by. Did anyone know what they were thinking?

"Until this year, in fact, I hadn't been able to write in about ten years."

"What is the censorship procedure? Do you have an actual bureau of some kind like the Russians?"

"Censorship?" he asked, looking at me with clear, unclouded eyes.

"Well, you don't just sit down and write whatever comes into your head, do you? There is a censor, isn't there?"

"No. We have no bureau like that."

"How does it work, then? Let's say you conceive an idea for a book."

"I discuss it with the Writers' Union."

"Why?"

"To let them know how long it will take me to write, and what the subject will be, and so forth."

"Why do they have to know?"

"So that I will not be assigned any other work and so that I will continue to be paid while I am writing the book."

"I see. And are they likely to discourage you if they don't approve of the theme?"

"Oh, no."

"But let us suppose, for example, that something in your story tends to contradict the current line, would they try to obstruct your writing the book? Or would they punish you if you went ahead anyway and wrote it?"

Unperturbed, his happy smile in no way altered, he said, "The truth will ultimately win out. It doesn't matter if it is suppressed for a time."

"But it matters to you, doesn't it, if your book becomes impossible to write?"

"Oh, yes, it would matter to me, certainly."

"Then what do you mean—that it would not matter to history?"

"Oh, yes, it would not matter to history. The truth cannot be destroyed. No one can do that forever."

"And would that be enough to reconcile you to a book being aborted?"

He sighed, but not tragically; it was all very remote. The truth, it seemed now, was that he could not really imagine himself writing such a book in the first place. Whatever in the past had caused his detention, he was certainly no dissident spirit any longer. He was ensconced in time and the new optimism, if one could call it that, and the Gang of Four was an aberration whose repetition in the future was not his present concern.

"How are you paid, Ai Xuan?"

"It is about two-to-seven cents per one thousand words. It is very low; we must raise it. But the Gang of Four eliminated royalties altogether. All writers were paid the same, even if they did not write."

Su Guang interjected, "He meant Chinese cents." His sense of accuracy had been jogged.

"So it is even less than it seemed."

"Yes. It is very low."

"Writers are poor."

"I think so," Su Guang said. Before this trip he had never met writers or thought about them. The writers he thought about were all dead, most of them for centuries.

I happened to turn and saw once again the massive portraits of Marx, Mao, and Stalin looking down at the crowds. I said to Ai Xuan, "I suppose you're familiar with the name Solzhenitsyn."

Ai Xuan looked blank and Su Guang asked, "What name?"

"Solzhenitsyn."

"Oh! You mean the Russian who ran away from the Soviet Union?"

"No, they expelled him."

"Yes, I've heard of him," Su Guang said, and explained it to Ai Xuan, to whom it was interesting news. But now for the first time an uncertainty showed in his eyes.

"He exposed the Stalin prison-camp system," I added, and Ai Xuan nodded but said nothing. Su Guang was also silent but was clearly having an ideological struggle with himself and it was not a simple one, given the proximity of the great Soviet leader's fifteen-foot-high portrait. "He wrote a number of books about it. Stalin destroyed a lot of people, you know."

Su Guang, admirably, I thought, commented without the slightest inflection, "We think he was a real revolutionary."

Ai Xuan said, "When Stalin was alive they sent us many valuable things, but afterward they only sent junk."

"Stalin probably shot more revolutionaries than Chiang Kai-shek," I said. "Did you know that?" I asked Su.

"We think he was seventy percent good and thirty percent bad."

Here in the Nanjing park I thought back to our second night in

Peking when a fellow American, William Hinton, had showed up toward midnight. If I hadn't talked with him, I would now be convinced that, unlike Russians or other peoples, the Chinese were unlikely ever to generate a dissident literature. But, in fact, Hinton said that he had read the first pages of a novel circulating in type-script, an underground book that depicted, in a wildly surrealistic style, an attempt on Mao's life by people who could only have been working for the Gang. It was written when they were still in power, and would have meant the worst for the author had his identity been discovered.

Hinton, who had spent thirty years off and on in China, seemed to be unsurprised by the existence of such a novel. That there are opposition factions and tendencies is taken far more for granted inside China than outside. At least this was so under Mao, when foreigners generally assumed a monolithic uniformity of thought which was more a propaganda picture than an actuality. China watchers in the West have so often been surprised by events inside the country because Western pragmatism inevitably seeks out the usable, finite conclusion, whereas the reality is a condition, a flux, many of whose elements are not even made public.

Indeed, it seems that the Chinese have a greater ability than we do to endure inconclusiveness. By Nanjing, I had realized that it may even have been an oversimplification to speak of "Mao's China," over the past years, when his line simply could have been one of a number simultaneously contending for dominance at any one moment. And, most important, that this condition was not considered to be disorderly. It was thus a dictatorship as far as the people were concerned, but one which was unable, or did not feel it necessary, to suppress all but the leader's opinion within its highest ranks. There might be imprisonment for holding the wrong political views and death for the landlord and "class enemy," but there may also have been more leeway for contention in the leadership than there was in certain American administrations, as for example, Lyndon Johnson's. Moreover, opposing factions at the top are reflected far down the ladder by lower-grade officials, who voice opposing views when it seems safe to do so. The monolith is of another kind than that in the Soviet Union, where the contentions on top are not nearly as openly projected down below.

But in any case, at the foot of the great stairway going up to the Sun Yat-sen Memorial, the writer who earned about two Chinese cents per thousand words, whose gray cotton trousers were thinned with wear and whose shirt was fragile with its hundreds of ironings, was not looking back at all. He had a book in mind to write, his pay scale was rumored to be rising soon, and, all in all, life was good.

"You look like a happy man, Ai Xuan," I said, as I noticed my wife approaching with the woman interpreter.

"Happy?" he looked at me with a particularly intimate surprise, and then gave a short laugh, "Yes, I am happy," as though it was an absurd question to ask a man who was among the living and with his prospects in view.

[5]

After only a few days I am beginning to feel the onset of depression, the product of frustration. It is not, as elsewhere, because I suspect we are being purposelessly misled, bugged, trailed by cops. Not at all. If the internal-security people are bothering with us, their discretion is exquisite.

Rather, it is the uselessness of attempting to understand and finally to arrive at some personal viewpoint about so immense a phenomenon, for what we are walking through is not merely China but the ranks of the survivors of thirty years of revolution, to say nothing of the wars since the mid-thirties.

For myself, I am frequently tempted to near-awe at Mao Zedong's actually putting into practice a concept of endless conflict *against his own bureaucrats.* And not merely to keep officeholders from accruing inordinate powers, but as much to give muscle to the people's awareness of its own right and capacity to change and create anything imaginable. If anything like this was true, Mao was the democratic apotheosis.

But then detail enters—detail, the curse of theory and generalization—and a much altered image begins to emerge. It has become impossible to believe that a "gang" or "faction " could have swung the People's Republic around its head without the consent and, yes, the direction of the Great Heimsman. The arithmetic will not let him off. For we are meeting people who were jailed and tortured in the mid- and late sixties, when Mao was vigorous enough to swim six and a half kilometers across the Yangtze River.

And there is something more that is depressing me. Foreign tourists and observers speak with near-envy of public order in China, in her streets and hotels, trains and airports. Her social discipline is unquestionably profound and in great contrast to the anarchistic selfishness, corruption, and crime that everyone laments in America and the West. In such a poor country one rarely hears of visitors attacked by stomach bugs, for China is clean. If there is nothing for a foreigner to do at night and no hot water in his bath about 20 percent of the time, he is likely to forgive the lack when he finds that he need not lock his hotel door to protect his belongings, since the young men at the reception desk on each floor are watching, and should he venture outside after dark, there is not a chance in a million he will be molested. A young American banker stationed for over six years in Hong Kong and touring the People's Republic

Inner courtyard, Peking

for the second time says, "I've worked in just about every country in Asia, and you can say what you like about Red China, but it's the only place in this part of the world that is absolutely not corrupt."

I am ready to believe him if only because I remember Su Guang's expression of conflict when I offered him a tiny bottle of medicine for his feet. Only after I had made him seem absurd for declining so monetarily valueless a gift, and one which I could offer out of pure human sympathy as a fellow sufferer from the same fungus, did he relent. But of course there is history behind his conflict about accepting a gift from a foreigner. There is fact—the obscene exploitation of Chinese by foreigners in the past, and there is the recent, purposely induced revitalization of the venerable phobic suspicion of foreigners by the Gang—or properly speaking, by Mao. Su among other things is a survivor. And indeed, in the sixties this sober young man was a student screaming his head off against the "capitalist roaders" in whatever position of authority. Now he smiles and once or twice laughs at some of the insanities of his generation.

But there is a subtler, evanescent cause for depression and it is one's Western need to nail things down; in China you are hammering on the surface of the ocean.

Where else is it possible to imagine this happening?: at the height of the violence of the Cultural Revolution, when Ba Jin, a famed novelist and already an aged man, was forced to kneel on broken glass before tens of thousands of onlookers gathered in a stadium to watch his humiliation, when people were being murdered, forced by the thousands to commit suicide, and when the *government itself would not intervene*—nevertheless, at that very same time, it did warn all concerned that whoever committed violence would face a "day of reckoning." In the latter part of 1978, eight and ten years later, trials were in fact being held and perpetrators of violence going to jail.

But—they were being sent to jail by a post-Mao regime which, there is no doubt at all, means to reverse much of his anarchic policy. In short, there is what one is tempted to call a long and impersonal Chinese fate operating apart from any particular regime's momentary policy; an anti-Mao government is punishing Maoists, but is carrying out Mao's threats against them. Moreover, it is frequently apparent that even among those wronged by the past decade's excesses there is no particular hurry to see wrongs avenged. China has plenty of time both behind it and ahead.

One is depressed, finally, by the image of a Mao which will not stand still within its outline. Some years ago upon reading of yet another pitched battle in the streets between "factions of the Cultural Revolution," I wondered—for the hundredth time—which of the factions Mao supported. And I thought of writing a scene.

Mao is discovered seated in an overstuffed armchair, center stage. There is a faint smile at the corners of his mouth. Two young revolutionists seated facing him on his right and left await a signal to speak. Mao turns to First Revolutionist, who proceeds to outline his viewpoints toward society and the world, and finishes by saying, "Comrade Chairman, my friends would appreciate your announcing that it is our view which is the true Maoist one."

Mao then turns to the Second Revolutionist, who at once launches into his ideology, which on all important points is diametrically opposite to that of the First Revolutionist, and ends by similarly asking to be awarded the title of True Maoist.

Silence. Mao, his faint grin still undisturbed, faces front. Both revolutionists sit tensely, leaning forward slightly so as not to miss the Chairman's least utterance.

Very slowly, painfully, and yet somehow inspiringly—the curtain begins to descend and Mao never gets to say anything at all, but simply maintains the state of tension created by the two points of view. Only one thing is certain and it is that *his silence is in charge*.

By the end of 1978 it still was.

To even begin to grasp what one is confronting in China and in Mao's unique methods of handling Chinese, perhaps the primary fact to absorb is that it was the historic feudal docility of the masses which had to be knocked to bits, exploded, chased away no matter by what means or under what slogans. Short of a self-confident people willing to believe in its own capacity to make great changes, nothing could happen. Thus, the concept of what in effect was permanent change. Of course the army was kept aloof, or rather refused to become involved and, in fact, opposed the Cultural Revolution in principle. Mao, however, did not demote the recalcitrant officers, probably remaining satisfied with being able to rely upon their forces should the aroused people get totally out of hand. This is following dialectic to the edge of the cliff.

[6]

In Peking only four days, I feel an intense need to talk to someone about the law, a subject in which no one in China seems to have the least interest. (In fact, however, within two weeks of our departure from China there were wall posters and demands voiced in demonstrations that the leadership adopt a new attitude of respect for legality.) If I were Chinese and did not wish to see my country losing another decade or two to anarchy, and more important, did not wish to be unjustly charged and punished for nonexistent crimes, I should surely look to law for at least some reassurance that the past would not return. But at the time of our trip China had not yet passed a legal code. The Party has the power to punish or let pass whatever it deems harmful or helpful to its rule and, worse yet, can change back and forth at will. It is government not by law but by political resolution, something understandable in a revolution's early stages but questionable, to say the least, after nearly thirty years of existence. There is a constitution, of course, but this cannot be more than a guide if beneath it is no codified law designed to make its provisions universally applicable.

Sid Shapiro came to China in the mid-forties, has lived there since, and is a Chinese citizen. In his sixties now, he translates from English and is fluent in Chinese. He studied at "the subway law school," St. John's University in Brooklyn, and was raised a few blocks from my family home in the Midwood section. His house in a quiet part of Peking is close to an artificial lake and the neighborhood is rather suburban in its somnolence this mid-morning. Three blocks from his house, not unlike some parts of Brooklyn, it is hard to find a passerby who knows where his street is, and as our driver squeezes down one narrow lane after another, I find myself staring out at the mamas and babies and the grandmas and grandpas padding around the neighborhood carrying a chair or a package or looking for a key on the ground and just being people, and I experience a vain longing for the day when it will be possible, perhaps a thousand years hence, to govern people by leaving them alone.

As Inge talks with his Chinese wife, a former actress and now drama critic, my fellow Brooklynite corrects my vision of things here. "No, there are no lawyers as private practitioners, but if an accused person wants legal counsel, he can get it. Most don't need such help because court procedure is simple and easy to understand. But they can and do call anyone they wish to testify or argue in their behalf." He is a man who is as enviably comfortable with his ideas as he is with his Hopje candy, only it has a Chinese name here, reminding me of Brooklyn, where this formerly Dutch, coffee-flavored sweet was the dentist's best friend.

"Where the hell'd you get Hopjes?" I ask.

"They don't know they're Hopjes," he confides. "They just make them. But aren't they terrific?"

We sit there chewing away in his rather somber living room. He had recently gone back to Brooklyn to see his family, but after an absence of thirty years, all he found impressive in America was the fear of crime. "They were worried as hell that I was going back to Manhattan on the subway at midnight. I couldn't believe it, imagine being afraid to go out of your house!"

"No fear here?"

"Not for a minute. These people are members of society."

"But don't they *ever* get out of line?"

He settles back and I realize we are into his favorite topic. We both unpeel paper from our Hopjes. I can see him clearly in Depression Brooklyn, cramming for his courses, getting good grades, turning his face from a failed economy, and feeding his soul on the Communist ideals of effortless justice. For injustice is not an inclination of humanity but something imposed by unjust conditions. Man is not only by nature good, he is most often Chinese.

"As Mao said, there are two kinds of contradictions: among the people, and between the people and the enemy. The courts don't involve themselves with the first kind of trouble . . ."

"Let's say a kid smashes a window, a guy beats up his wife."

"That kinda stuff never gets into a court."

"What about cops?"

"Rarely get near it. What happens, the neighbors lean on the kid and his parents to straighten him out. The peer pressure can weigh fifty tons."

"Like in Brooklyn."

Shapiro hesitates to agree—there should be nothing in China like anything in America.

"I mean," I continue, "that families were really the main source of discipline in those times."

"Well, in a way," he agrees, more politely than actually, "but here the pressure is not just sentimental, it's based on political principle."

Chang An Avenue, Peking

"To beat your wife is anti-Communist." And I suddenly thought of a line in a Depression play by Clifford Odets: "A man who beats his wife is the first step to fascism."

"You could put it that way, sure. But beating a woman is political since it cuts across the Party's position on women's equality, it's a feudal throwback."

"Gotcha."

"Stuff like that."

We both laugh at the revival in us of our ancient speech. "But what do they do with hard cases?"

"There aren't that many."

"But there have to be some."

"Well, in that case he goes before a judge and two laymen who know the defendant. And they struggle with him to reform his ideas. Crime is basically political, the result of reactionary ideas."

"Give me an example. Take theft."

"Okay. Theft is the attempt to consume goods without working or producing, so it is antisocialist and therefore a political act."

"That's very good." I am impressed.

"So political means are the only ones that can cure it."

"In other words, instead of moral inhibitions—"

"Which mostly don't work," he quickly adds.

"Why don't they work?"

"Because under capitalism you've got enormous crowds that don't have anything, while a few have a lot."

"So in a sense," I say, "it is politically correct to steal under capitalism."

"And even morally correct. They are righting injustice. But," he cautions, "you can't graft the Chinese system onto America because it is based on a just economy here. You can blame a man for stealing when he has a job and the chance to eat, but you can't if he's unemployed and starving."

It is the socialist lesson I first learned in Brooklyn Depression days, but Sid clearly delivers it like late news, and I find myself both marveling and irritated at the windless space he occupies where in truth nothing has penetrated in forty years. "But you really don't feel anyone needs to be defended once he's in trouble?"

There is a certain smidgen of defensiveness, not more. "But why! Before anybody's accused, the investigation is absolutely fair and thorough, and it goes on for weeks. Believe me, people who aren't guilty are never accused. The problem is never guilt, it's how to reform a person."

"There can't even have been a case of mistaken identity?"

"Well, maybe one in ten thousand, but that's not such a problem that you'd have to introduce lawyers into the system."

"But, Sid," I say, trying to smooth the anger out of my voice, "from my first minute in this country I have heard of nothing but the crimes of the Gang of Four, the thousands jailed without charges, without appeal, unjustly . . ."

"Yes, but that was not the system, it was the *breakdown* of the system! The Gang of Four *disrupted* the system!"

I was surprised that this particular kind of childishness could still start anger flowing in me. But there were millions like him all over the world who had managed to convince themselves that revolution could not and should not make men freer. Every eighteenth- and nineteenth-century revolution had at least declared the rights of the person to be the centerpiece of society and had sought to draw a line beyond which the state could not reach into the individual's life. Now only the state had rights and powers, and the person, like his property, belonged to the collective itself, and with no recourse or appeal if fools or factions should decide on his ruin.

Wang Fujing Street, Peking

But before one dismissed as routine propaganda Shapiro's insistence that injustices, such as those perpetrated under the Gang, were merely passing and uncharacteristic episodes rather than inevitable consequences of the system, one had to ask oneself the same sort of question about America. Does, for example, our veritable army of prisoners, most of them poor or black or both, define American civilization to an important degree? If I must doubt that Chinese justice works as blamelessly as Shapiro would have it, I know for a fact that American justice does not work in far too many instances. We do indeed treat the big thieves far more tenderly than the little ones, and the lawyer available to the poor is almost never as competent or as eager to win as the lawyers of the rich, and so on.

As well, if peer pressure often can turn Chinese youngsters away from criminality, it can also become the tyranny of the majority over any nonconformist opinion. But what we call individualism in America is often a rootless condition in which families lack the human contact that can solve problems before they reach the courts. So it may be that formal protection of individual rights when totally divorced from the realities of social and economic inequality is indeed empty legalism. But it hardly follows that the abandonment of such protection is the key to a just society. Shapiro's position begs the question no less than the American one, which supports the construction of additional prisons but not a radical examination of the system's tendency to produce new prisoners. The issue, it would seem, is how to sustain liberty and, at the same time, ample social and economic opportunity, rather than to justify the absence of one or the other.

With our disagreement in the open, it struck me that this moment was emitting the same opaque quality that frequently arose with Chinese when any principle was up for discussion. Shapiro must surely be disturbed, if only remotely, by a society without law, in effect, but a revolutionary cannot display his own uncertainties, let alone allow them to be part of a discussion. So it was once again not so much a cultural barrier I felt warding me off in China—Shapiro and I could not have been culturally more alike—but a political creed whose fundamentals must not be so much as examined, most especially in the presence of those not of the faith.

"I'd like to leave you with one instance of what I mean. I got involved," I said, "with a murder case in Connecticut some time back; a teenage boy was arrested, tried, convicted, and sentenced for the murder of his own mother. He wasn't black, Jewish, a hippie—nothing but a majority boy arrested by majority cops who simply had grabbed the wrong suspect. But the police and political bureaucracy could not and would not admit it was wrong and did a cover-up for years, told more and more lies, fabricated evidence, and so on. We finally got the kid freed, and with the help of lawyers, Sid."

He muttered something about the remote possibility of errors, but we were leaving now and I regretted my foolishness at having argued at all. After all, he was powerless here, especially as a foreigner in China. As we drove away down the quiet Peking back streets, maze-like and narrow, I felt their ancientness pervade the car. And the thought returned that hardly more than 10 percent of Chinese lived in cities, and that "out there" was the vast majority, bent to the earth as it had been forever. And I recalled that in Russia it had not been very different, this tendency to go dead before the question of man's separateness from government, his right to alienation, actually, from which sprung his critical intelligence and defense against tyranny. With its nearly religious expectation of the human community reborn, was Marxism the true successor system of capitalism or feudalism? The distance to post-Renaissance parliamentary capitalism is truly vast, but to feudalism it was amazingly close. Feudal man, like man here and in Russia, "owed" much to the group, everything, in fact. Under this socialism he could not move his residence without permission, for he was "part" of his commune, his factory, his social organization, and every single one of the nearly billion Chinese, like the Russians, was a member of what in feudal times was called a guild and here a collective—of doctors, dentists, workers, peasants. Looked at this way, there was indeed no place for lawyers, for the very concept of an individual standing apart from the group was no longer possible for the mind to contain.

And it had happened too, I recalled, in another place and another time. The Puritans also forbade lawyers, and I had even given to Judge Danforth in *The Crucible* a response to the very mystery I was now turning over in my head. "The pure in heart need no lawyers," he had assured the complainants who had come to beg him for counsel to defend their loved ones against the charge of witchcraft.

And there as here, it was not mere cynicism that drove intelligent men to embrace and celebrate their own vulnerability before injustice. It was the age-old dream of unity, of sonship and daughterhood, of the trustingness of family transposed into social relations. And all of it by virtue of a high belief in the state's sublimity, in the Society of Saints in Massachusetts and socialism here. One might smile at its naïvetés, but not at the morale it so often imbued its believers with, and the feats in war and construction it rallied them to perform.

The Puritan theocracy lost its monopoly when surpluses of food and goods undermined the earlier need for a near-military unity that justified the suppression of conflicting ideas. Has the time approached for China when suppression, for analogous reasons, no longer appears as justified as it did when the Japanese Army still occupied the country and a feudal Chiang Kai-shek had yet to be pushed into the sea?

[7]

Just outside Peking there are three plants building electric generators. In 1958 there were none. But telling the heroic story, the plant's propaganda director and his two assistants, none of them over thirty-five, are not visibly inspired by their tale. In fact, they look at us worriedly as the outline fills up. "The workers built this plant at the same time as they built the first dynamos themselves, production started before the roof was on. They came, about six thousand of them, from all different kinds of jobs and places, and trained themselves. It was the Great Leap Forward of 1958 . . ."

It is clear as one watches the small man who is speaking from the edge of his one-place sofa that he is approaching the bad news. It is obligatory, in 1978, to blast the Four, and he delivers the general accusation: "They demoralized the people."

"Could you give me examples?"

"They went among the workers and told them they were supposed to work against the leadership."

"Work against them how?"

He begins to look even more worried. "To disobey the leadership's authority."

"But why did the leadership stand for this?"

He stares at Su Guang's face for a long moment before turning back to me. Then his gaze drops to the floor. Evidently for him, as for others, this is part of the dream, the nightmare whose torn webs are still sticking to their hair. Why indeed was a merry band of maniacs allowed for so long to wreck a society?

By this time, if I still lack the answer I have at least a stronger suspicion that it has to do with faith, indeed a faith bordering on the religious in whose grip they could not have affirmed the law of gravity had Mao repealed it as a bourgeois obsolescence. But it is only partly embarrassment to them now. Sitting there watching the three, I sense that they are uneasy at telling a foreigner the truth, baldly, undefensively, and, it seems to me, admirably.

"I am a writer," I tell the propaganda director, "and I can only explain about the Four with examples. I would appreciate all the examples you can think of. Stories, you see? People understand stories better than general statements."

He nods. He approves of getting the news abroad, and it is to be understood that the followers of the Four have not been shot but still move about society in their tens of thousands. Once again it is clear that the propaganda director's function at this moment is to do what he can to cut off the maniacs' road back to power.

Reception room, factory for generators, Peking

We leave the formal sitting room with its compulsive symmetries obviously designed by the Soviets: two lines of sofas facing each other, mathematically placed tea tables, and the symmetrically hung portraits of Hua Guofeng and Mao. There are moments, in such rooms, when one wonders if on each end there walk a precisely equal number of flies. But there are no flies to be seen in China any more.

Out on the production floor one notices that the machines come from Shanghai, Germany, Russia, and Sweden. Nothing, however, is spinning, the twenty or so workers sprinkled down the three aisles being occupied with looking occupied, it seems to me. Or is it lunchtime? I forbear to ask the propaganda director. I smile at a worker and he seems surprised and smiles back. Some of the milling machines and the big lathe are familiar to me from the Brooklyn Navy Yard shop nearly forty years ago and I confide this fact to the propaganda director. He looks back at me with a certain flaring of the eyes, and nods, and makes his confession, now that I have apparently noticed how outmoded their equipment really is.

"We are technically about in the mid-fifties."

"That's too bad."

"Yes."

We walk about, Inge photographing turbine blades, beautiful structures of concentrically bladed fans.

"But now we will begin to catch up."

"Can you tell me what happened here?"

We have halted at the wide-open door at the end of a bay, the blue autumn sky over our shoulders. The propaganda director has yet to smile. After a lifetime of induced suspicion of foreigners, he is having to adjust to telling me his country's weaknesses. I think, as he speaks, that if these people are capable of adapting even to telling the truth, what can ever defeat them?

Factory for generators, Peking

"In '70 and '71 we had many young workers in their teens. The first thing they were taught was anarchy."

"But who taught them that?"

"The cadres of the Party."

"Taught them not to obey anyone?"

"More—to contradict whoever told them to do anything."

"For example."

"If they were assigned to polish a piece of metal they would refuse and say, 'I want a different piece, I don't wish to work on this piece.' "

"Actually?"

"Oh, yes."

"And what would happen then?"

"He would be ordered a second and third time, and when he refused, his work group would stop work and discuss his action."

"How long would that take, an hour?"

"Two weeks, a month. Longer sometimes."

"You're not serious."

"Oh, yes."

I recalled a Chinese former actress, now living and working in New York, whose troupe had been ordered to stop performing and went into a period of mutual confrontation and "struggle" which had lasted for three years. During that time the company had done absolutely nothing but talk to one another until every last detail of every one of their lives lay wriggling on the floor. Among many other things, the Cultural Revolution was a nation indulging in a confrontation with itself that lasted something like a decade. The purpose of it all was to drive out, by exposure to the group, every last shred of selfish ambition, elitism, superiority, but finally, as it turned out, the urge to work at all. There cannot have been anything like it in history.

But I had always assumed that a vital industry like this one would have been spared, but apparently not at all.

"And how," I asked, "would such a case be settled?"

"Sometimes they would decide that his right to work had to be suspended. Other times it never got settled, just ignored for a while till it boiled up again."

"But how did anything at all get done?"

"The veteran workers, the older ones, never approved this anarchism. You see, the younger ones thought it was their turn to be revolutionary."

"They'd had it too good."

"Oh, yes. They had never fought the Japanese or the Chiang Kai-shek reactionaries, so to disobey in the factory they thought was heroic. In 1973, I imagine you've heard, the Zhang Tiesheng incident occurred."

"What was that about?"

"A student handed in an absolutely blank examination paper for entrance into the Agricultural Institute. Zhang Tiesheng instantly became the hero of the day all over China."

"Encouraged by the government? That is what I don't quite understand."

He took a breath. We were verging dangerously close to Mao. And finally he said, "Encouraged by the Gang of Four."

"And this plant is owned by the government, right?"

"Certainly."

"So the government was encouraging sabotage of itself."

He nodded. "The Gang of Four . . ."

"Right," I said, forbearing to press him.

"There was also," the propaganda director continued, "the case of Huang Shuang. She was a primary-school pupil who fought 'teacher's dignity.' "

"What is 'teacher's dignity?' "

"It is the tradition in China that the teacher has always the final word, the dignity. Huang Shuang also became a great heroine for her decision." For a machine shop it was terribly quiet, I thought. "Of course they were most often the worst students who did these things—refusing to study or take examinations. But the worst of it in this plant was the disrespect for the Masters."

"Master Machinists, you mean?"

"Yes. When they came in the morning, instead of saying 'Good morning, Master Chang,' they would say, 'Hey!' "

"Right." I nodded, trying to recall how we had greeted our Master Machinists in the Navy Yard. It was more or less "Hey," I suppose, but there was really no analogy. "Master" doubtless had feudal, slavish implications for the Cultural Revolutionary and America had had no feudalism to threaten us.

"And instead of learning from the veterans they lounged around and talked and let the veterans do all the work. So a whole generation of young workers never learned very much and just smoked a lot of cigarettes."

"And what about now?"

"Oh, now the veterans are happy." I glanced down the aisle of the bay we were standing in and the workers may indeed have been happy, but it did not seem to me they were doing very much work. "The leaders now dare to lead."

"No horsing around any more," I said.

This took Su Guang an extra half minute to explain to the propaganda director, who savored the expression, which brought on his first smile. "That is correct, no horsing around now. 'To grasp class struggle and make great order in the land' is now our motto, as Chairman Hua Guofeng has stated, plus the Four Modernizations, which . . ."

Once more we were off to the races, the slogans dropping out like jackpot nickels. "But tell me," I interrupted, "in all honesty, do you think the Cultural Revolution did any good? I mean, do you think it is more democratic in this factory than it was?"

He seemed a bit nervous and defensively said, "We now have one to two mass meetings a month. That is more than we had under those people!"

Still, one had to wonder whether "those people," cracked as they undoubtedly were, had not added a little something to keep the revolution honest before they had themselves slid into a tyranny of their very own, the tyranny of the young, the inexpert, the ignorant, and the self-righteous.

"And what will happen to our country," Mao asked seven thousand Communists in 1962, "if we fail to establish a socialist economy? It will turn into a . . . dictatorship of the bourgeoisie [that is, of the new class of technologists and experts], and a reactionary, fascist dictatorship at that."

The Cultural Revolution was launched to invigorate the "below," the underclass, the will of worker and peasant. If its survivors were to be believed, this thrust for democracy had created instead a fascism, with torture, mass denunciations, and industrial chaos. What element or principle had been omitted that might have kept the movement true to its best self? For the truth was evidently something far more than the depredations of the Four; one had only to recall that every artist we had so far talked to still held the initial conceptions of the Cultural Revolution in near-reverence.

Those precepts call for nothing less than a democracy in which quite literally every living human would share with every other in the Kingdom, and none any more would be high or low, and the first would be last . . .

Shaking the propaganda director's hand in farewell, I could imagine the mix of anxieties in his breast. Had he done the right thing or said too much and revealed weakness that an enemy would seize on? Could a foreigner understand that what had first pranced onto the scene like a pure white horse, and was still remembered as such despite everything, would return again someday to China, flashing its beauty and its promise, and that it was still a mystery why it had turned into an ugly monster trampling on everything?

[8]

As tales of the past decade's confusions piled up day after day, a remark Frank Coe had dropped seemed to move closer to the center of all the possible explanatory ideas. "Mao didn't believe he had to wait until the forces of production matched the relations of production."

Every businessman knows that his firm's capability to produce comes first; his machines and processes must exist before he can, for example, hire labor. Surely there must be available housing in his area, transport, water supply, and so on. The forces of production, men and machines, certainly precede all else.

Mao thought otherwise. Properly motivated people, people imbued with creative and self-sacrificial Marxist concepts, could, in effect, gather on an empty plain and make steel, glass, cities, and whatever else their minds could imagine. He did not believe that China had to wait until a technological infrastructure was in place before launching herself into producing what she needed. Thus, as we saw, the workers had built generators at the same time the factory was being constructed and did not wait until it was finished. Likewise, steel could be made in back yards, and was made, as well as all sorts of primitive but often ingenious machines.

The Gang of Four went even further, not only laying total stress on the relations of production, but also chasing away, beating to death, or driving to suicide those who had achieved expertise in any field.

What is more interesting, however, is the breadth of support for this leveling among the Chinese. (And, one might add, among the embittered sons and daughters of the upper bourgeoisie in Europe and the United States.)

After even a little time in China, the mid-sixties and seventies take the shape of a rising wave which at some point broke and crashed upon a beach. Doubtless to spare Mao no one is willing or able to give a precise date, but at some point Mao's idealistic and inventive concept of a totally creative population was transformed into a weapon against anyone who had by that time achieved anything that might entitle him to social privilege.

Was this distortion the idiosyncratic act of a frustrated woman, half mad with envy and the fear that as Mao weakened she would be discarded by the powerful men around him? (The common belief is that the leading Central Committee members demanded and got from Mao a promise never to put Jiang Qing forward as a political figure—before they would support his marriage to her. She took vengeance on them all.) Or did it represent a deep strain in the Chinese who had been enslaved over the millennia by classes of "experts," the scholars and intelligentsia who had only contempt for work and workers, and knew how to manipulate them? Traditionally, as in any feudal society, the holder of even the slightest state power, be it only the job of postmaster, gathered around him a clique of sycophants, and these together humiliated and exploited the mass. Through a Cultural Revolution not only were the members of the "expert class" to be humiliated and driven off but the class itself was to be eliminated. Nobody was ever again to be in a position to lead anybody; it was, in effect, to be a body without a head.

But regardless of whom I asked whether this indeed was her vision, I received only the same shrug. No projection at all of a future had ever been announced by the Cultural Revolution, and no one believed that Jiang Qing and her clique had ever actually thought ahead that far. Had Mao? Or had it all been a vast improvisation through whose wreckage we were now picking our way and trying to put together noses, limbs, fingers which in fact had never been connected in a form at all but had been dropped where we found them, helter-skelter, everywhere one looked?

One thing at least seemed reasonably probable—the specter whose coming all this had been set in place to prevent was obviously the technological civilization of the West and Russia, with its substrata of anomie and cynicism, its spectacular atomization of humanity into private units, neurotic, self-absorbed, and rich with all the soul's diseases.

If this was true, one had to sympathize at least with Mao's motives, for as the world progresses it seems to die. The mystery and wreck of Maoism, consequently, must reach out to many minds far beyond the Middle Kingdom.

[9]

It is hard to believe we've been in China less than a week. The outside world, the "real" one, has been closing down for me. So it is a fine thing to hear an American voice again.

Near midnight, Bill Hinton shows up, a big blond man with a self-deprecating chuckle and, despite his ruggedness, his thick neck and broad limbs, a look of deep tiredness.

Hinton is the author of five books on China, among them *Fanshen*, which I had avoided reading for years, thinking of it as a formidably detailed and, I imagined, zealous apologia. But I was all wrong. Once begun a few days before leaving for China, it became a daily point of reference, and for Inge as well. Hinton had found himself, in the forties, right in the middle of typical peasant life in the Liberated Area, and personally took part in the struggles within the peasantry to drive out feudalism and establish socialism on the land. Surprisingly, the book, like a novel, is filled with personalities, individuals groping for a lifeline out of the darkness of the feudalism the Reds had smashed. Among other things it is a detailed story of life at the bottom, sometimes a day-by-day record of the attempt to make everyone in the village equal, right down to the number of pots and pans in each house, to say nothing of the size of their landholdings. Its candor inevitably has drawn the condemnation of many radicals abroad, but it is read by Chinese, whose own writers have yet to produce a work truthfully recording the revolution.

Hinton had gone to the Far East from Cornell. His mother had established the Putney School in Vermont. Now he operates a one-man farm of four hundred acres in Pennsylvania. He has spent a total of ten years in China, he figures, and has been going back and forth for the past thirty. He seems a worried, mystified, but not hopeless man now. Indeed, China is the apple of his eye, and if he criticizes, it is to save her from herself.

"I've got to get home next week to bring in my corn. I wasted a couple of weeks with pneumonia out there in Shanxi. Probably'd got better sooner, but all these folks I used to work with in the forties kept coming in to give me advice how to get better and bringing candy and all kinds of stuff I couldn't eat. I hardly got any sleep." He laughs with love and pride, but the look of preoccupation never clears from his eyes.

"We've been hearing all about the Cultural Revolution . . ."

"Oh, Christ, yes." He keeps nodding for half a minute, trying to decide how to say what he wants to say, then sighs. "I don't know how to tell you . . ."

"It has all the earmarks of mass hypnosis."

"That could be." He ventures forth now. "I know for a fact that there were instances of people literally crucified against walls in some places, nails driven through their palms, and left to die . . ."

But if for him the good in the Cultural Revolution could never be overwhelmed by its excesses, the memory of them still seemed hurtful. I change the subject. "What are you up to here this time?"

"I'm the consultant on the land-reclamation project in Heilong-jiang."

"Is it working out?"

"It will, I think. They're pretty good at that kind of stuff."

I try to make light of it, and laugh. "You sound a little doubtful."

"No, not about reclamation. It's the mechanization of the land that's the problem. They just took delivery on a million bucks' worth of John Deere tractors; the John Deere engineers didn't think they needed those giant machines at fifty grand apiece, but the Chinese insisted, and they shipped them, and when the Deere people saw fields as big as two thousand acres, they were surprised but relieved."

"Will they know how to operate them?"

"Oh, they're quick learners, they'll do that okay. But the way to get food out of spaces like that is to let the machine do what it was designed to do. But they're not trying to slow down an influx of people into the area. They'll defeat the benefits they could get from mechanization. You don't *want* tens of thousands of peasants loose on open land like that, not if you've got the machines to exploit it. They'll slow it down, they'll bring it to a halt. I produce, all by myself, plus machines, more corn on second-rate Pennsylvania side-hills than a Chinese brigade of more than four hundred people. They're creeping up to a billion population, they can't afford that kind of misuse. The problem is the continuation of past practices— too many people were sent into the area in the first place, and now as they try to rationalize production there's a bad problem of displacement. And on top of that, the newly opened lands are being populated at the same rate as the old—about three hundred workers to seventeen hundred acres. One hand doesn't seem to know what the other is doing. One farm has American equipment replacing ninety percent of the workers while a few miles away they are oversettling land at the same rate as before. The result is that they don't really mechanize and they themselves consume a large part of the grain they produce. Where they could be building a modern Manitoba or North Dakota they're building a Shandong. It's the tremendous tendency of any society to re-create itself."

"I guess they don't know what to do with all those people."

"Exactly, and I don't either, but this way is not the answer." He shakes his head, snorts, rubs his palms into his blond hair. "It's so damned hard to change a tradition," and in China that tradition was to overwhelm usable land with people.

I am trying my best to suppress my interest in the crucifixions he had mentioned. Meanwhile . . . "I see they've got a lot of these walking tractors . . ."

"Oh, yes, they're turning them out by the thousands now."

"I have one myself in Connecticut . . ."

William Hinton

"They're really not much good for field work, but the Chinese use them a lot for transport and pumping—a portable power supply— and I guess they're useful that way. But they don't really do much to mechanize agriculture."

"I notice them all over the roads."

"Sure. Even their fifty- and sixty-horse big tractors are mostly hauling freight on the roads, 'cause that's how they can make the quickest buck."

"I'd have thought there'd be a more rational use of machines than that. More control from above . . ."

Walking tractor

He smiled. "I wouldn't be too sure the control from above is always all that rational either." Then he laughed. "They had me looking over some of their new tractors, basically the clumsy old Russian design. And I noticed they didn't have any drawbars . . ." (The drawbar is a heavy bar of flat steel bolted to the tractor's rear end for the purpose of pulling a plow, mower, or other implement. All the pulling forces of the tractor converge on the drawbar, and a tractor without one is like a rake without teeth.)

"How do they pull things, then?"

"From the three-point hitch," Hinton said.

"But that's for lifting and pulling *mounted* implements. Don't they break it?"

"Sure do. The Vice Minister of the First Machine Ministry heard me out and called in his engineers and said, 'Why don't we have a drawbar on our tractor?' Well," Hinton went on, "at the end of a lot of discussion it turned out that they had never designed their tractors with drawbars because there were no trailing implements in China to pull. I argued that people couldn't invent trailing implements because there were no drawbars to attach them to. It came down to a stalemate and the Vice Minister lost his temper."

"That is sad."

"Yes, it is."

"So what are we really talking about?" I asked.

"Well, for one thing, the way they separate design from practice, because that's what this is all about, and right up and down the society. It's part of their feudal burden, which is so damned difficult to throw off.

"I was in a tractor plant around Tianjin once not long ago, and I got on one of their machines to find out why it had such a wide turning circle. A decent tractor should turn on its own wheelbase, just about, by braking one wheel. It's important in maneuvering in the field.

"Well, I braked this tractor and all its innards protested and I thought it was going to bust all its bearings. I tried another one and it was the same thing—sounded like it was rupturing. The Vice Minister was watching with all his engineers and they were depressed by the racket. I noticed they had an old Massey-Ferguson there, probably the only one of its kind in China, which God knows how they got hold of. And I mounted it and swiveled it around right and left like a kiddy car. And the Vice Minister was impressed.

"So he asked why *their* machines couldn't turn like that and the engineers looked a little sheepish. Then he asked his head engineer, 'Have you ever driven a tractor?' And he hadn't. Then he asked the second engineer if he'd ever driven one—well, of course none of them had so much as mounted a tractor and there they were designing them. I mean, this is real life."

"But wouldn't they have even been curious enough to . . . ?"

"No, no, the point is that driving the machine was a manual thing to be doing, and they are not and do not want to be manual workers. The fact that I've got a university degree and worked for eight years as a truck mechanic, and that I farm—these are incomprehensible contradictions to them. And it's that in feudal China no brain worker ever so much as touched an object with his hands. It declassed him. In this case, the Vice Minister ordered every one of them to learn to drive a tractor within a month and it was a revolutionary idea."

"Discouraging."

"It is, but that doesn't mean they're not going to make it. They will. They're going to make it, but it's going to be a long time."

We sat in silence for a moment. Suddenly he said, "I'm an American nationalist."

How strange that sounded from a man who had given so much of his life to another nation's revolution! But it was hardly that simple. He was really trying to help the country he loved to contribute her genius to those who so desperately needed it to create a new way of life. While nations still existed, one had to admit to being part of one's nation, just as no one could truly be, as the ultraleftist slogan would have it, "All public, no self." Calling himself a nationalist was a blow at abstraction, one among many that he hoped would work to break the awful circle of illusion and disillusion among Communists, a process of idealization which so often ended only in the absurd and the ultra-left. His lust was for the concrete—"If you don't love the American people, how the hell can you love the Chinese? As I see it, internationalism is based on nationalism, just as you can't have a collective without individuals. People are forever ending up in limbo, attaching themselves to some ideal motherland where utopia has already been built, until it turns out otherwise. You have to have your feet on your own ground first before you can take on the world. Otherwise, you have no means of judging what is good and bad in other places and other revolutions."

"Were your people farmers?"

"No. At least not for generations. They were English, New England and Midwestern professionals."

"I keep asking the same question and getting no answer. It seems to me after this recent disaster here somebody ought to be thinking about law. About some independent point of appeal from injustice, even if it's only some agency within the Party . . ."

But an independent judiciary, he felt, was a peripheral problem. It was really the sanctity of property and the respect for property rights that webbed the system together and underlay what security civil liberties enjoyed in the United States. "In the last analysis one's property rights are upheld because anything else threatens the whole system. It's not because the judiciary is independent, which it isn't, but because property is still fairly widely dispersed, and this creates a multiplicity of interest and viewpoint, and a certain independence. All wealth has not yet been monopolized. Not that an independent judiciary isn't vital.

"The problem under socialism is that there is no power other than state power. In the U.S.A. real power lies with big wealth and state power serves big wealth. Wealthy people pop in and out of government, but generally prefer out to in. In China this is not so. If you're not *in* you are nothing. This makes power very unstable. In the U.S.A. wealth passes from one generation to the next in the same families. Presidents come and go and so on, but power is stable. Not so in China. A change in regime in China means somebody goes up and somebody goes down.

"I can't see a possible base for an independent judiciary in China. When push comes to shove, what would make it stand up? But in itself that is not so important, I think; what is important is civil liberties, the right to speak out and to create." From his words and his eyes, and however concrete he was trying to be, it seemed that the whole question of coexistence, of liberty, creativity, and socialism had yet to be settled for him anywhere.

"I guess you speak Chinese, don't you?" I asked.

"Not great, but pretty well."

"Do you find a kind of veil between them and you?"

He thought for a moment. "Not with peasants. I get straight answers from peasants."

"They're not afraid to talk about the system's failings?"

"Sometimes. But mostly they come right out with it. You see, there's no way of demoting peasants because they already are where you're 'put down.' " He smiled.

"The land is punishment."

"For some intellectuals and city people, unless, of course, they go to the country to make points in a career record. But the peasant knows he can't get any further down so he's not afraid to talk straight. It's different in Peking, for instance, with any official people. The indirection is enough to make me dizzy. I can't get close to them. They make an art of evasiveness. For one thing, nobody wants to be the one to make a decision he can be blamed for later."

"Do you understand what happened here in the past ten years?"

"I do not. And I doubt anybody else does."

"It sort of all goes soggy when you think about it, doesn't it?"

He stares ahead for a moment, then looks at me. Something profoundly hurtful is in his face. "It often happened, you know, that they'd suddenly come out of nowhere . . ."

"Who?"

"People. Thousands of them around a leader. A leader nobody'd heard of before. A new warlord, young, sassy, who didn't give a shit for anything or anybody—right out of some factory somewhere, and behind him his own staff, runners, trucks, arms, even concubines. Right out of the tenth century, including the contempt for the peasant, the kick in the teeth . . ." The hurt in his eyes is simmering. "They were unknowns in many cases who had only been employed some place for a few months, but they'd emerge as powerful leaders able to mobilize hundreds of thousands of followers. The worst of it was to see how quick they were to tear at each other, to humiliate anyone handy. That was the worst of it, seeing that again, that awful desire to grind somebody into the earth . . ."

A pause. An air of helplessness before evidence he insists he cannot suppress, above all perhaps from himself.

"They had a real civil war going. Heavy artillery battles. Thousands of people were killed . . ."

"What I still find hard to grasp is, what did Mao make of that chaos? I mean, he was still there, right? And still functioning . . . ?"

Hinton shakes his head, grins at me. "He said both sides were wrong."

"But made no move to stop the fighting?"

"Oh, no—he said, 'Argue, but don't fight.' "

"But they *were* fighting. With artillery, even."

"Yes, that's right. But it had gotten completely out of control."

"So what'd he do?"

Hinton looks down at his hands, then back to me, shaking his head. "Nobody understands this, Miller. Not yet. Maybe it's too soon."

"I wonder sometimes if Mao wasn't actually playing with the idea of obliterating the state. Letting the changing currents rule for as long as they could, until they in turn were overwhelmed by some new concept, until finally after a lot of blood and God knows what chaos—there would be a democracy."

Hinton nods for a moment, shrugs. "I don't know. Nobody knows."

Chang An Avenue, Peking

"You don't agree with my idea."

"I probably don't, no." He stretched out his legs and rested both hands on top of his head. "I did a study, *Hundred Day War*, about the Cultural Revolution in one university, Qinghua."

"I haven't read it yet . . ."

"You might look at it. What I found was that after the first weeks of struggle, all question of political principle really collapsed. What you finally had was simply a power fight between leaders. There was no moral or political content any more, simply the egos. This is what our American radicals simply can't digest, or the ones in Europe, I guess. And it's why I'm attacked so much. But I was there, and I saw it, and that's how it was."

"You don't have to sell me. But let me go further. Do you think this kind of protracted turmoil was a kind of substitute for a system —which doesn't exist here—a system to transfer power to new people within an institutional framework? In other words, does the feudal class system reassert itself time and again because, in effect, there is no legal sanction to slow it down?"

"I'd have to think about that. It's possible."

"And that's why you keep getting these wild swings—from hard authoritarianism over to anarchy and back again. It's all a groping for, so to speak, the watercourses down which the power can flow back and forth, instead of breaking loose and flooding the landscape. But I have to add," I went on, "that what is unique here is that these swings are still possible within a dictatorship; it's very hard really to contain the phenomenon within any normal ideological framework."

"You probably don't know about this novel that's going around in typescript," Hinton said, quite suddenly.

"You mean like *samizdat*?"

"I'm not sure." He corrected himself, "I mean, I'm not sure whether it will continue to be suppressed." And corrected himself again, "Or even whether it's just being left to dangle from some bureaucrat's fingers for the moment. Anyway, there's no author's name on it and it's typewritten, and it opens like this.

"A woman is rushing across a bridge one winter's afternoon. Clutched to her breast is a sick, dying infant, and she is dragging a reluctant six-year-old by the hand. She stops passersby to ask for the nearest hospital or doctor, people direct her, she is half hysterical as she rushes along. Suddenly in the middle of the bridge, which carries both rail and ordinary traffic, the six-year-old catches hold of the railing and hangs on, won't go a step farther. She pulls at him, screams at him, slaps him, but he won't let go. Finally, she leaves him and rushes off with her gasping infant.

"A few minutes later an armed guard appears. Mao's train is supposed to pass over this bridge at any minute and they are sweeping the area to protect him. The guard sees the six-year-old and tries to move him along, talks to him but gets no answer. Deciding to break the child's grip on the railing, he discovers its hand is made of steel. He reaches under the sleeve and finds a steel arm. It is a robot bomb. They disarm it just as Mao's train approaches the bridge."

"What an opening! And then what happens?"

"I don't know. That's all I read."

"And which faction is supposed to be behind the bomb?"

"Lin Biao's. But there is an additional symbolism, too. The robot implies the technological mastery of the armed forces, particularly the air force, which is seen as distinct from the other spheres of Chinese life."

He stands and rolls up his denim work jacket in one hand. "I've got to get ready to leave, start getting my corn in."

We shake hands. He waves to Inge, who has been trying to keep awake on the bed after sixteen hours on her feet today, taking pictures. "It's terrific you speak the language, Inge. It'll help a lot. They'll be flattered you took the trouble. Good luck."

At the door he turns and laughs. "I say a lot of negative things, but I don't want you to get the idea that . . ."

"I understand."

"The revolution is loved by them. Don't ever forget that. It's their pride and their dignity and all their hopes rolled up together. Nobody here is yearning for the old system, which was organized stupidity and perpetual disaster. But there's going to have to be a lot of bad habits changed and a lot of hard truths faced before they can move on ahead. With nearly a billion out there, they don't have a minute to waste, you see?"

"Not ten seconds, sounds like."

He moves out into the hallway and walks off in a long-striding lope, still tired from his illness. What seems to set him apart is not so much his profound investment of work and hope in another country and its revolution—others had done likewise. Rather, it is the absence in him of the contempt so many rebels bear for their own culture and their own country's character and institutions; he seems not merely to have displaced one idealization with another— or one disillusionment with another to come. What Hinton seemed to be proposing was on the order of a tragic activism that entailed a kind of persistent patience before the facts of experience. No nation's future is knowable, and in any case cannot be grafted onto it from another's history. The present is but the leading edge of a long and particular past whose failures, confirmations, and denials reach deeply into the personality and self-conception of each people. To lay upon that complexity the abstractions of political theory, without at every step of the way correcting for errors of fact and experience, is to lock a society into a mirage of unreality which travesties any claim to a scientific viewpoint. He seemed remarkable, too, in his not being some quondam American more at home in China, more in love with a farther shore. Perhaps he is the bearer of an unfamiliar kind of consciousness for whom the past is not a mistake to be denied and exorcised and thus left to repeat itself so insistently that it overwhelms the future. If he has been humbled by the Chinese experience of the past few years, he seems also to have resolved to remain with the battle. It had been a long haul and, clearly, he saw that it would be longer still. The blockers had thrown themselves at him not only from the American yahoo right, but from the left, too, and would doubtless continue. But if he was committed to any prophetic hope, it had to embrace the mastery of concrete, operating detail; the paradox of human need bound to the human resistance to change is never broken otherwise. And in this he was perhaps preeminently American.

[1 0]

Yanan is China's Valley Forge. Dusty and dry, with wind-worn mountains and arable land only along the watercourses, not unlike parts of Arizona. To this remote fastness Mao, Zhou, and the military chieftain, Zhu De, led a ragged thirty thousand and camped after the fabled Long March, a strategic withdrawal to escape destruction by the superior armies of Chiang Kai-shek. They lived in caves gouged out of the loess mountain walls, just as the locals in many cases still do. After eleven years here the army had grown to 300,000 people, who had converged from all over China, from cities and countryside, men and a few women fed up with Chiang's corrupt regime and his impotence against the Japanese occupation. Possibly the key to this army's phenomenal growth lay in its fundamental instruction never to accept even food from peasants, but only hot water. The peasant since time immemorial had been the victim of every army that happened past his house. Yanan, in fact, was one of China's first Liberated Areas and the first spot of socialism in Asia.

There is some industry now but the plan is to turn the Yanan area into the consecrated shrine of the revolution, with its central attraction the four caves where Mao dwelt in those chancy years, living, it must be said, with Jiang Qing at least some of the time. Here, too, Edgar Snow made his way to become Mao and Zhou's closest foreign friend and confidant, and their movement's explicator to the Western world. It was also in Yanan that I caught cold and, a day later, Su Guang, too, leaving Inge to tour the relics and Mao's caves alone with a local young woman interpreter named Zhao Suping who had the build of a discus thrower and the determination to go with it.

Zhao Suping, twenty-five years old now, came of age during the turbulence of the Cultural Revolution. It was her time. She does not volunteer attacks upon its theses or personalities. Alone with Inge she says quite simply that she is not interested in being close to anyone. It seems not merely a personal, idiosyncratic remark after those years of commitment and what must be for her the current disillusion. She is a tough and resourceful girl.

A low fever and too many impressions have sunk my spirits, but sometimes it is useful to force oneself to observe a place in a discouraged mood which, no doubt, some of the indigenous population normally share. I stand outside our hotel on the main street. The pavement is broken, rutted, being excavated here and there for a sewer pipe. The fog of burning charcoal, the dust, the cold frontier sky, the endless line of bicyclists that seems to stretch the two thousand miles from Peking to this outpost, the dark doorways from which a chicken saunters or an old woman carrying a tiny chair on which she sets a doll-like granddaughter of three.

Now down the street marches a troop of about twenty children six or seven years of age, their schoolbooks in sacks strapped to their backs, all spiritedly singing together, doubtless some revolutionary ditty. Surprisingly, there is no teacher or adult with them. They have simply collected somewhere and—it is now about seven in the morning—are marching to school all by themselves. Seeing me, they break off singing, and without losing a step burst into applause as they pass before me. I applaud back. Recalling the many reminders that a year or two ago we would have been shunned as foreigners, it must be that they have been instructed, these six-year-olds, to applaud when they happen upon a barbarian. The discipline of China is formidable, but nevertheless the children are undoubtedly happier applauding than staring at a stranger with hostility.

Children clapping for foreigners, Yanan

Inge has bought me a thermometer in the pharmacy. Entering, and asking for it in Chinese, she collected a crowd of women who at once spread out on the counter all the dozens of identical thermometers in the stock to pick out for her the one with the prettiest and least marred red cardboard case. Inge's impression was that it may have been the first thermometer actually bought by a foreigner in the history of Yanan. One can imagine how for weeks to come she will be talked about as the foreign tai tai who bought the thermometer. It cost about ten cents.

Later in the day Su Guang hands me the Chinese herbal medicine against colds which he has been taking. It is a black licorice-looking ball with the consistency of taffy and the smell and taste of camphor. Eating it, one ceases to concern oneself with one's cold, since all one's psychic forces concentrate on not throwing up. Su claims to be recovering, but he doesn't look too hot to me.

Nevertheless, we rally ourselves to accompany the much stronger women, Inge and Zhao Suping, out into the country for a visit to the Cadre School, but not before I have looked in through a window on the Yanan street at a shop where some fifty women are working at sewing machines, making the inevitable Mao–Sun Yat-sen jackets. Having worked for a while in my time in New York's garment center, it seems to me these women are not as quick and dextrous with the machines as the sewing machine people I once knew. But they were all fanatics in those Depression days, paid by the piece and pushing the seams through at the needles' highest possible speed. Lunch for them had been a bowl of sour cream with an onion cut into it and a fistful of pumpernickel bread; it lasted fifteen minutes. Delicious. One of the workers, Louie Kurtzman, would bite off the threads at the end of each seam until, by afternoon, his lower lip was covered with bits of rayon of half a dozen colors, like whiskers fanning out of his mouth, and since he smoked cigarettes down to the last three quarters of an inch there was a low-level apprehension that Louie would burst into flame.

Tailor's, Yanan

The Chinese women were far more relaxed, chatting easily as they lined up their seams under the needles, pausing frequently to make a conversational point. But their dismal shop would not have been possible in the garment center even in the thirties. A few dim fluorescent tubes cast a spectral light and were hung overhead at random, leaving dark shadows over some of the machines, and the workers were densely crowded together besides. It was more like one of the Lower East Side sweatshops of turn-of-the-century New York, or the non-union underground dens employing illegal immigrant workers now. Watching the women through the window reminded me of something Hinton had mentioned about the technical level of Chinese farming: "It is roughly at about the level of the American settlers in the early 1800's." Yet, for all one knew, these Yanan garment workers were filled with as much hope as American garment workers had been when life was all work and work was life.

The significance of what we saw at the Cadre School took several days to penetrate the cold in my head. To the naked eye it was a collection of large farm buildings set in roughly the form of a square, with an immense threshing floor the size of a basketball court in its center. About thirty young men with a dozen or so women, wearing protective masks and wide-brimmed peasant straw hats, were working at whirling husking machines which spewed out rice kernels to then be tossed upward by men with wide shovels and winnowed by the fast currents of air driven by large electric fans at the edges of the threshing area. A few of these workers glanced at us as we appeared, but not with any apparent intensity of interest. Some surreal emanation did touch my fevered mind from the sight of these peasants—there was a distinctly un-peasant-like air about them. Probably the absence of any older

Hulling rice, May 7 Cadre School, Nanniwan

people may have accounted for this, I thought, but in any case I dismissed the feeling and dutifully trooped through the repair shop and storerooms where once again the youthfulness of the help seemed unusual.

The clue should have been evident with the young woman doctor, who was an M.D. not a "barefoot doctor," in the whitewashed cave used as an infirmary. She and the middle-aged director of the school enthusiastically demonstrated the homemade operating table by raising and lowering its hinged ends, which could set the patient in any desired position for examination or for an operation. And she did operate, as she said with an eager smile, and had already done an appendectomy on the admirable table. I thoughtlessly informed her that I at that very moment was running a low fever, the best news she had had in a long time, apparently, for she sprang at once to an array of wooden drawers, from one of which she counted out fourteen yellow tetracycline pills, screwed a little sheet of paper around them, and handed them to me. With throbbing head I tried to listen to the director's spiel; as I should have realized, the "peasants" we had seen were actually Party workers from cities who were here to study Marxist theory while working with their hands in order to understand what it meant to be a peasant. Many of them had high positions, but here they were ordinary labor, as we could see for ourselves. One of their main texts was Stalin's on economics, but possibly their most important task here was to absorb the Yanan tradition of revolutionary self-reliance and living-for-the-people. Sometimes whole masses of youth walked forty-five kilometers here in symbolic imitation of the Long March, which of course had stretched some eight thousand miles and taken years to complete.

Now Inge, in Chinese, asked the doctor about herself, and the latter, like the smiling director, was delighted. She did not know how long she would continue to work here in the cave. Actually, she came from Xian, this province's capital, and had been here about a year. Without the slightest air of having been under criticism, her eager grin and bright eyes quite untroubled, she said, "I am here to change my world outlook."

Operating room, May 7 Cadre School, Nanniwan

It would be days before it dawned on me, as the result of a conversation in quite a different place, that like the "peasants" in this camp, the doctor was here to be "re-educated." Had they been followers of the Gang who now had been forced to change places with their former enemies, people who had been stuck into cadre camps for years to get *their* world outlooks straightened out? I confess it had never occurred to me to ask, most probably because there had not been the slightest sign of the doctor being under duress. As well, the camp's director had even emphasized the ideological purpose behind the camp. Whether some or all of the personnel were under arrest, in effect, or volunteers, was impossible to tell from the structure of the place; there was no surrounding wall, no barred building, and the barrack-like living quarters, while Spartan, were as decently comfortable and airy as peasant houses in the newer commune settlements. But even during the Cultural Revolution such camps had held detainees under the same conditions—and, indeed, in those days some people often volunteered for re-education. In some cases, they were allowed to visit their homes once or twice a week. I suppose it is a matter of taste whether such arrangements make the whole business more sinister or less.

Of course the question, and one for which there is still no answer, is what the real feelings of the occupants of such places are. One had to recall another of Hinton's remarks: "The young are pretty skeptical now . . ." It would seem inevitable after what had been so totally right turned out to be so utterly wrong.

But there would be occasion to learn as days went by that part of Mao's legacy was the endlessness of struggle, the concept of the ever-present Two Lines; you might be right this year but detrimental the next, or vice versa. This is unreal to an impatient Westerner who needs to arrive at "truth" in order to die for it or live with it in his pocket. A Westerner's "truth" is a finished product which becomes part of him and his moral personality.

For Mao, only the struggle is permanent and the closest to truth one can come is to recognize and admit to necessity. It takes bravery to recognize necessity and act accordingly; to do what one has to do can mean shaking up one's whole life, hurting old friends and breaking hallowed obligations in order to make oneself into an instrument of history. The alternative is nostalgia and moralism, and paralysis before the needs of the hour.

The young doctor and follower of the Four need have no remorse about the damage she may have done in the past, provided she understands what she must think and do now. Guilt moves no stones.

It is a long view and a muscular philosophy eminently fit for a world where nothing stands still long enough for one to touch it. I suppose it is a pragmatic idealism, the Chinese version, if you will, of the old American business philosophy, or, for that matter, the commonly held philosophy of nations which, as the saying goes, have no friends but only interests. Stripped of sentiment, it is the American creed, in a sense, or was when we still had the arrogant self-certainty to worship practicality. It was left for Old Europe to forbear tearing down ancient buildings to make way for a factory or parking lot; for us nothing was sacred but progress, construction, change, newness, and each dawn severed America just a little more from its own past.

Undramatically, even blithely, a seventy-five-year-old theater director in Shanghai who had spent over ten years in confinement would remark, "When the next Cultural Revolution comes . . ."

"There will be another one?"

"Oh, many, certainly."

And just as the young doctor in Yanan showed not a sign of remorse as a former Four follower who must have committed some outrage to warrant her detainment now, the elderly director would show no bitterness at all toward his captors. Indeed, we happen to know one of his captors, who now lives in America and has immense affection for him, as he does for her. It may be, in fact, that things do not end in China at all, ever.

It may be worth recording now—in the little time left before the construction of the Intercontinental and Hilton Hotels makes such a scene impossible—the pig slaughter ten yards from the Yanan hotel.

While Inge and Zhao Suping were off to Mao's four caves, I lay trying to doze in our room when the pig began crying somewhere out beyond my window. It was impossible not to try to see what was happening, and once outside I could trace the cries to a nearby wall of filigreed stone. Through the open spaces I could see three men who had thrown a gigantic black pig to the ground. One man had a foot-long knife in his hand. They were studying the operation before them and I could not bring myself to watch.

But even yards away the variations in the animal's squeals were strikingly expressive. On hitting the dust, there is a high-toned, rapid outcry of indignation, "Yu-ee! Yu-ee!" for he has been living at peace with people for so long that this rough treatment is an outrage.

But when he finds that he really can't raise himself against the force of the men's hands, the first shriek of fear enters his voice, and this becomes even more piercing as his dainty feet are tied together, and the sound is intolerably human as his jaw is stretched up to await the stab of the knife. It now becomes a duty to turn and see with my own eyes. A glance through the wall is enough— the knife tip is just entering the tough skin below the jaw, and as the blood trickles out, the pig begins to plead to be given one single moment to explain who he is and how contented he has been feeling since his flanks and hams filled out with fat and solid flesh, and how much he has been enjoying his life. And he naturally imitates the human voice in order to get sympathy. I turn away.

And now all his life fills his voice, an astonishing awareness of all he has been and possessed and is so unbelievably being torn from, and I have to turn back again and look, and I see that the power of his pleading and his protest, the force of his awareness is enough to make the men's restraining arms tremble as though in this crescendo they had unexpectedly recognized a fellow creature. For an instant this is confusing to them—but the honor of the man with the knife, which the sudden heave of the great pig's hulk has caused to slip out of the already bleeding wound, is an honor enraged, and his two helpers rally against the pig's appeals as though it were now their kind against his kind, and the long knife is thrust inch by inch into the vibrating throat and the pig's last voice sounds like, "Oh, oh, oh!" and he experiences his darkness.

The men stand looking down at the motionless, immense body on the flattened dust and they are still breathing hard. They were doubtless well acquainted with this pig, which has roamed the yard for months. For a long moment they do not move as they stare down at it, the struggle over. It is as though they must observe this little interval of stillness to permit the departure of a chilling unity with the great black dead thing on the ground.

[1 1]

The chief conductor of the Xian-Shanghai express carries his immense importance with professional ease. He is the "Responsible Person" on this train, the Man Himself, equivalent to the captain of an ocean liner or chief pilot of a plane. He is not your average Conrail ticket puncher who may or may not be able to turn up the air conditioner. The chief conductor here knows every rivet of his train. And he is not shy. He bows slightly as he slides open the compartment door and enters with a dignified but warm smile on his round face, his blue uniform of light cotton spotless and well ironed.

He is making the rounds of the few compartments with foreign passengers, like the chief officer of an ocean liner after the first day out, asking if we have any suggestions for improving the service.

"It is difficult to sleep in this compartment," I say, "because there is very little air, and if one opens the window soot comes in or a big draft."

He seems surprised and not too happy to hear this and points upward at two circular air vents. "Those are all open."

"Maybe they are, but nothing's coming through them."

He sits down on one of the couches and his expression seems rather defensive and I am fairly sure he is not accepting my criticism.

Outside, the rice paddies are gorgeously green, now that we have passed out of the Yanan aridity and those bony mountains, and the peasants here, up and about with first light, are chopping and hauling, spreading night soil among the plants, or riding on little trailers behind the two-wheeled walking tractors. I have yet to see a tractor actually working land, but it is usual for a dozen or more peasants, men and women shoulder to shoulder in a line, to be slowly chopping their way across the landscape as they hoe a field.

The chief conductor's eye has fallen on Inge's broken-backed Chinese grammar book, and he takes it from where it lies beside her, asking what she is doing with it. She answers in Chinese and a great grin breaks out on his face and he is full of questions about her interest in the language. "I will fix your book for you," he says, folding his hands around the dog-eared volume. And now he turns to me and says, "I regret about the air but the vents are really all open."

"I'm sorry too, but there is still not enough air."

"I will look into the problem."

Now we settle in for our talk. "How old is this train?"

"It was built in 1956."

"It's practically new, then, by American standards."

"Fairly new."

"Russian design?"

"Yes, that was all we had then. We must design new ones, especially with air conditioning."

"You like air conditioning?"

"Oh, yes, air conditioning is very, very good. It is the most important improvement you can possibly have on a train."

"I agree."

"Have they given you enough hot water and tea?" He picks up the thermos, weighing it in his hand.

"Quite enough, thank you. How is it to be chief conductor? What are your worst problems?"

"Well, of course the equipment is quite old now. We must have new equipment. But we are building five new railroads and we must wait until those are all finished and running. You did not sleep very well last night?"

"That's all right. I haven't slept well since we got to China."

"That's too bad. Why?"

"Chinese people love to collect under hotel windows to have loud discussions at two o'clock in the morning."

"Really! You must complain."

"I suppose they're busy doing something important. In two hotels now they were moving steel beams around in the courtyard all night."

"Yes, but we are building all the time, you see."

"I have no doubt about that. What other problems does a chief conductor have? Are there ever thieves on trains?"

"Oh, yes." He smiles contentedly. "There are many."

"Really! What do they look to steal?"

"Whatever they can lay their hands on."

"Even under socialism?"

"Some people still have the habit." He makes a grabbing motion with one hand. "But we have our security people always on board."

"Police on board?"

Chief conductor, Xian-Nanjing-Shanghai express

"At all times. They deal with these people very well. They rarely succeed in stealing anything."

"And besides stealing? Are there ever collisions?"

"Not since the Gang of Four was overthrown."

"How did they cause wrecks?"

"By organizing struggle against discipline."

"Could you be more specific? How did they organize struggle against discipline?"

"Many ways. One way was to start a discussion among the workers just as a train was about to leave the station. They'd delay one train, then another, until a pileup was inevitable in all the confusion. The servicing of the equipment broke down for the same kind of reasons."

"But I should think it would be to their interest that trains not crash. And who could conceivably gain from such confusion?"

He looked at me to be sure I really was so naïve. "But you have heard of their slogan."

"Which one?"

"Better a socialist train that arrives late than a capitalist train that comes in on time."

He laughed at the ludicrous idea and I asked, "And nowadays is there any ideological work going on on this train, or are you purely interested in efficiency?"

"There certainly is ideological work. We are always educating ourselves as Marxists. There are Party members in our crew."

"How many?"

He counted in his head for a moment. "Nine out of forty-three crew members. I am the head of our Party branch—" He suddenly broke off, noticing a volume of Tang poetry in Inge's carrying net. Asking her permission, he took out the book and totally lost consciousness of me. "Where did you get this?" he asked in surprise.

"In a Peking bookstore."

Arthur Miller, train ride, Xian-Nanjing

"I did not know it was in print again." And again he seemed to lose himself in the poems from that most glorious era more than a thousand years ago. With excited eyes he turned to Su Guang to ask what Peking store this had been found in, and Su informed him, and regretted that he had not accepted a set of two volumes which Inge had offered to buy for him—for a dollar or so. The Tang poems, some of the most admired in the language, were prohibited by the Gang of Four in another attempt to wipe out memory of the Chinese past, with the excuse that they were feudal and slavish and glorified only the rulers and their running dogs.

But as both Su, a reader of classics, and the conductor doubtless were aware, this was by no means the first regime in their history which had attempted to wipe out the past by burning the books of former dynasties in the hope of obliterating their influence.

For ten minutes or so Inge, Su Guang, and I sat silently as the chief conductor, his face enraptured, turned from poem to poem. Then, as though refreshed, he stood with a happy sigh, thanked Inge for letting him see her book, and backed out with her beat-up grammar in hand.

We are taking this twenty-hour train ride because the planes from Yanan to Shanghai go only three times a week. But on a long run trains are good places to meet people, however sleepless the nights. In the short run, though, they are hell, and I must walk up and down the corridor beside the compartments to try to distract myself from the boredom. Through the glass panes I can see that the other compartments are filled with Japanese men who are touring this part of China. Some are old enough, it seems, to have taken part in the Japanese occupation of this area of China forty years ago, but their Chinese guides seem to be enjoying their company, chatting away, drinking tea, bursting into loud laughter now and then. And indeed my inquiries so far have all been answered in the same way—the Chinese blame the old Japanese militarists, not the Japanese people, for the murderously long war.

After observing so many Japanese shepherded by Chinese, as well as the greetings in hotel lobbies between technical delegations of both countries, it is obvious that the Chinese manner is far less inhibited, formal, and artificial. It reminds one of their respective theater styles, the Japanese being comparatively understated, noble, and from a Western viewpoint rather humorless and unearthly, while the Chinese is demotic, loud, garish, funny, and careless about piling farce onto tragedy. Even millennia-old Chinese sculpture is often laughing openly rather than mysteriously smiling in classic Buddha fashion. And, in fact, the Chinese sense of humor seems to adore outrageous absurdity, not unlike the American in at least that respect.

I would never have believed that I could be so taken with Chinese opera, and Chinese theater altogether, the realistic plays less so, however. In Chinese opera the artificiality is so honest! And I was completely unprepared for the dominating roles of the women characters. In *The Women Generals of the Yang Family* the last male in the ruling family is killed in battle, so the women have to take over the generals' posts and lead the armies against the enemy. It is a very old opera, too, not something recently cooked up to fill out a quota of women's-liberationist theater pieces. In fact, the prominence of women in all the Chinese theater we saw led me to theorize to Su Guang and two other Chinese men present at the moment that perhaps there had been a matriarchy in the distant Chinese past which the operas were unconsciously recalling. Su Guang, to my surprise, did not at once understand the idea and I had to explain the meaning of matriarchy. Like the others, he looked simply embarrassed for me, incredulous that I could pos-

Su Guang, train ride, Xian-Nanjing

sibly have so much as thought of such an idea. Women running a country! I had to warn Su to watch out lest he turn into a Bad Element for his male chauvinist thoughts, but between laughs he clearly did not think he was in any danger on this count, the idea of a matriarchate being beyond all discussion.

Even in the so-called Traditional Play that we saw in Peking, the central concern of the story is a woman who, to keep the peace, is required to separate from her family and marry the prince of a hostile and distant border tribe. She bears the prince's children and in time learns to love him, whereupon she is commanded to return home, again for reasons of state, once more uprooting her life. The prime minister who is responsible for these cruel orders is traditionally shown as a nasty villain, but in the current version written by Guo Moruo, a prolific author who died in his great old age only a few years ago (and is often rather sneered at for his easy shifts of public enthusiasm for any currently dominant political system or line), the prime minister is farseeing and wise and shares the heroine's anguish. It is he who makes it clear that her sacrifice is heroically justified by the peaceful development it guarantees for China and her near neighbor.

The play's theatrical interest derives from its knockout sets and costumes and the fluency of the stylized acting whose authority even the foreigner must instantly recognize. (And incidentally, Brecht's debt to this kind of theater as well as to Peking opera is clearly immense.) The wide stage is swathed from left to right in a broad band of fading color reminiscent of Rothko—a painter, needless to say, unknown to them. Addressing one another, the actors extend both arms forward, while resting one hand upon the back of the other, a seemingly ancient noble gesture of polite greeting and a very convincing way of documenting the feudal strangeness of the era. But backstage after the performance the actors told me they had invented the gesture, stolen it from an old painting, in fact, and were delighted that it looked so authentic. So much for learning one's history in the theater.

The object of opera acting, and to a lesser degree that of the traditional theater, where there is no singing, is to behave on stage as differently as possible from the way people do in life. No entrance is made in opera in a straight line, always in sweeping curves, often accompanied by the clacking of wood blocks in the orchestra with each of the actor's steps. Likewise, finger and hand gestures are all curved. There is a complicated etiquette involving the use of the long sleeves which hang down to the actor's calves. The women seem to punctuate indignation by swiftly swinging their sleeves around and around until they twist up tightly around the wrist, the motion timed to conclude with the end of a speech. The men raise their sleeves by tilting the forearm upward and allowing the sleeve to slide back, revealing the hands, especially when they are plotting some evil, or trying to appear to be in deep thought.

Makeup is never used naturalistically, always to enhance the artificial. Long beards hang in a straight line just under the nose, concealing the mouth—rather like a vertical mustache, in fact. The faces of the women are very pink, and they of course speak in a high nasal singsong, and walk in a kind of short-stepping trot even over a distance of two feet, the jiggling motion reminiscent of the hobbled, bound-footed one which was found sexy in the old days. (Explaining the reason for binding women's feet, Su Guang affected ignorance of its sexual connotation and saw it as a means of preventing women from leaving the house. I wondered how they managed to work in the fields with crippled feet and Su claimed that in fact they rarely did. Occasionally, it is still possible to see such women, all no younger than their late fifties now. Their feet look as though the metatarsal arch has been compressed from front to back, so that it forms a kind of clubfoot.)

The idea of tragedy seems totally alien to Chinese theater, but not necessarily tragic feelings in the course of a tale. Informed that her beloved husband has been killed in battle, a wife bows her head, turns three quarters upstage, and, raising her left hand to near shoulder height, rapidly waggles it for a moment in a signal to the audience of her inner distress. Then, without of course actually touching it to her face, she passes a scarf just under her eyes, sparing makeup but also maintaining the illusion of her separation from ordinary humankind. It is sometimes very close to the acting in our own silent films, but it is surprisingly affecting, nevertheless.

What is really incredible, however, is the juxtaposition of the sublime and the ridiculous without its creating any evident sense in the audience of a violation of stage logic. A woman tells a man some dreadful news, he listens intently, seriously, and suddenly does a back flip in place and goes on listening to her as seriously as before. His is rather a booby character, however, and I could only imagine that by convention each character behaves to suit his own nature rather than conforming to a consistent overall comic, tragic, or romantic style.

It is a show-and-tell sort of extroversion, this style, even to the point where a woman entering carrying a tray of tea things sweeps down to the edge of the stage to show all the nice silverware to the audience, then carries it up to the table where it belongs. Like Chinese life, it is a style without privacy, the actors turning to the audience whenever an important point, a complaint, or for that matter an exclamation of success is to be made.

Like classic drama everywhere, it is filled with analogy involving relations between power and man, state and individual, and is never very far from its teaching impulse. And like the structure of the Chinese language, the scenes are usually compact and follow each other without transitions, story points coming bang-on one after the other as required. The audiences either know the stories or have heard them sufficiently often to be interested not so much in what happens but in the style with which the expected is performed.

The heroine of *The White Snake*, for example, is played by three different actresses, one for each of its acts, not only because the role is so strenuous, but also because each act demands a different strength in a performer. In the first, her singing is lyric and complicated; in the second—for which everyone waits with high anticipation—fantastic acrobatic skills are obligatory; and in the third, the dramatic ability to create a woman of grave dignity. The greatest opportunity for novelty would seem to be in the acrobatics of the second act, which were absolutely astonishing in the production we saw. The heroine is attacked by spears thrown from *four directions simultaneously*; she hit them back with her elbows, hands, hips, and *ankles* over at least a five-minute period, each spear returning to the hand of its thrower who, moreover, is as often in motion as standing still. She made the Harlem Globetrotters look like cripples. Of course, the effect is magnified by the orchestra's banging away on everything that can make a noise and in so fast a rhythm that the image on stage was of a woman gloriously caparisoned in glittering silver cloth firing spears out of her body almost effortlessly, borne on waves of sound and light, a woman radiating colors and spears.

A performance of *The White Snake*, a Kun-style opera (more lyrical than Peking opera and more of a chamber piece, they say), intrigued me with its immensely suggestive symbolism and stymied any attempt to deduce a consistent subtextual story. But it is one of those very old and beloved works that will doubtless provide an endless source of contention for anthropologists and the psychoanalytically inclined once it becomes available to Western stages.

The mere attempt to summarize the story fell to pieces soon after we had seen it, quite as though there were some inner clash of realities which the onlooker's mind both took in and was incapable of holding together afterward. More, when I tried to get a summary of the plot from New York friends familiar with it for many years, they also lost their way in it despite their initial certainty. Combining my own impressions with Inge Morath's translation of the precis as given in the theater program, plus the recollections of our friends, the following is the story of *The White Snake*. That is to say, it is the story before it begins to blow apart in thin air like an old mushroom.

On the Fifth of May all creatures feel uneasy; it is the day of the Duan Yang Jieh festival, when every living thing feels the urge to return to its original form. (Not that *The White Snake* was created to "illustrate" this idea or to explain why we sometimes feel that we

West Lake

aren't really ourselves. But at the same time nobody denies that maybe this is what lies behind the whole thing.)

A thousand years ago in Sichuan Province, where, just as today, the E Mei Mountain stands, a magnet for all sorts of fairy folk, the snake fairy Bai Si Jian, the White Snake, descended from heaven. ("White" means plain or simple, an understatement in this case.) She was accompanied by her sister, the Green Snake, or Little Green Snake. In some versions she is blue, but it does not matter because "Xiao Qing" means the color of nature and can be either one. Or black, which is another story. Green Snake, in any case, is White Snake's handmaiden and assistant, and the actress playing Green Snake is all business, rather like the private secretary of a film star, certainly far less dreamy than the one playing White Snake. But both are gorgeously got up in satin pantaloons and turbans with yard-long, spotted brown spear-thin feathers, exactly like those on the goddesses in the temple at Foshan.

The White Snake

White Snake and her sister arrive in Zhejiang Province near Hangzhou at the shore of West Lake. (The itinerary of these fairies is as exact as if they were real dignitaries.) It starts to rain and they naturally look around for somebody who will lend them an umbrella. In their search they run into an umbrella owner named Xue Xien, whom, after carefully considering him for an aria, the White Snake decides to marry. The husband, wearing a lovely brown velvet gown with enormous sleeves and a chic tubular hat with an overhanging flat top, is poor. Since Chinese opera of any type is dominated by the female characters, who have all the dignity and weight of leadership, Xue Xien is inevitably a bit of a booby who sings in a high, girlish voice. (Nobody in our row knew for sure whether he was played by a man or a woman.)

The wedding is accomplished with a wave of Green Snake's finger, after which she expects White Snake to return with her to their home in heaven. Actually, by the rules of the cosmos, they are supposed to remain on earth only for a day. But White Snake has fallen in love with Xue Xien and insists on continuing life together with him. Green Snake, as with most things her sister gets excited about, could hardly be less enthusiastic, and her singing gets very whiny and complaining. She is militant, correct, brave, and rather a nuisance to her lyrical sister, whose fantasies are limitless.

The newlyweds move to Jiangxi Province, where White Snake practices medicine and her husband sells medicinal herbs. (Naturally, her real identity is concealed and she goes under the name Bai Si Jian.) Business is good and they are getting along fine. But not for long.

Fa Hai is the Buddhist Superior or Chief Monk of the temple on Golden Mountain and a horrible-looking old man. He "represents feudal forces" (according to interpreter Su Guang's whisperings into my ear. But one ought not jump to the conclusion that the purpose of this opera is to attack feudalism. It does attack feudalism—a remarkable target in 1978, if one thinks about it—but one is entitled to doubt that that is its sole or even main purpose).

In any case, Fa Hai has learned of the Snake-Demon's descent to the earth and her marriage to a mortal man, an out-and-out violation of every rule of heaven. On top of that, she is daring to cure illnesses and sell medicines, really intolerable actions akin to throwing a lighted firecracker in front of a man standing on his head. For to offer sick people medicine is to interject materiality when they should rightfully meditate and burn incense to exorcise sickness. Therefore, on every imaginable count White Snake (whom the Superior naturally calls "Demon") is a big enemy of Buddhism. (All of which may persuade some people that this play is an attack on mysticism and a defense of scientific method, and it may be. It probably isn't, however.)

Xue Xien

And so, convinced that White Snake is a menace to the human species, the Buddhist Superior comes to husband Xue Xien to inform him that he has married a snake. Naturally, Xue Xien doesn't believe him. In every conceivable way his wife is a normal woman and he would as soon drop the whole subject. But the Superior gives him some special wine, called Xiong Huang, which, if his wife will so much as sip it, will reveal her real shape. Xue Xien wants neither the wine nor the advice, but once the old, horrible-looking Superior has left, he has both and can't rid himself of either. A man who is told his wife is really a snake is not going to forget it easily even if he finds it unbelievable.

Now Duan Yang Jieh Festival Day arrives. White Snake is not feeling well. Xue Xien looks her over and concludes that she is pregnant. They are both exceedingly happy, and husband, in his excitement, pours his wife a drink of you-know-what. But she refuses. He offers it again and she refuses again. They are singing and singing, and she is holding her belly and looking wan and he is offering the glass, which she takes from him only to put it down again, and he picks it up and passes her the glass again. The actors handle all this magically, easily, stylishly. And finally she takes a sip, but not "dramatically," only as a kind of favor to him and in a passing sort of way, as though she might well be unaware of exactly what kind of wine it is.

She goes into the bedroom and he sings by himself for a minute until he peeks into the room at her and falls down dead on the floor when he sees what's on the bed—a white snake.

This is soon remedied by White Snake, who immediately climbs to the highest peak of Kun Lun Mountain and finds the sacred mushroom which can revive the dead. But not before she has a fine balletic mini-war with guardians of the mushroom, all male, whom she vanquishes, as the women always do in Chinese operas. She returns home, revives her husband, and once again they are on the verge of peace and happiness.

But husband Xue Xien, true to his foolish nature, feels he should go to Golden Mountain to burn incense and thereby guarantee the future good fortune of his family. No sooner there, he is captured by the awful Superior in order to keep him from ever rejoining his wife. But undaunted, White Snake, with sister Green Snake at her side, goes forth to search for her lost husband, whom she traces, inevitably, to the Buddhist monastery and the evil old Superior. She demands Xue Xien's freedom, singing at Fa Hai, the dreary abbot, with impressive indignation, the tones rising and falling like the whine of a saw.

Unable to budge the old bigot, she summons up a tribe of underwater fairies who live in the Yangtze River, in order to confront fairies who live in fire, whom the Superior commands. In the ensuing fire-against-water ballet, the stage undulates suitably like the elements the fighting dancers personify. Now the river fairies cover the whole mountain with water, and in the midst of this victorious flood White Snake feels her fetus move, and growing weak with the oncoming birth, she has to beat a retreat.

(At this point it seemed to be a creation myth, one written by women. Unlike the Jewish-Christian serpent, this snake is good, plain, and simple, rather than dark, devious, and malevolent. All the trouble—presumably in the cosmos too—begins with the interference of an old man, who incidentally represents the priesthood, and who breaks up a happy and fruitful marriage on a technicality —that the woman is not human, a not uncommon way males have of looking at females, at least as women tell it. Which is probably correct.)

While this battle has been going on, husband Xue escapes the monastery with the help of an outlandishly clownish monk, the comic figure of the piece. Sending out growls and groans of laughter from behind dense, waist-length whiskers, hooting and jerking his head in a duck-walk and winking to the audience, the funny monk leads husband Xue down the mountain toward his home. But just as the latter is feeling the relief of the saved, he sees before him his wife, White Snake, and worse yet, her sister Green Snake, who meet him on the Broken Bridge. (So named because in winter the snow does not stick to the crown of its arch so that the path across it looks broken. It is still there on West Lake, of course, rising from a causeway which forms a lagoon. In fact, it was near Broken Bridge, during a solitary walk one evening, that I discovered couples snuggled, one pair to a bench, all along the lake, while parked beside each bench was a pair of bikes. The experience settled some questions about Chinese courtship.)

The two snakes proceed to take apart husband Xue for his ineptitude, stupidity, cowardice, emotional irresponsibility, desertion,

The Little Green Snake

fatuousness, whining incompetence, and a number of other minor and major character deficiencies which fill out the sisters' duet, perhaps the most passionate in the piece.

Xue, in reply, now announces that even if his wife is a snake he will never again turn against her or listen to gossip. Despite this humiliation, sister Green Snake still did not look satisfied, at least not to me, but the couple return home, and for the third time, by my count, are on the verge of living happily. With joyful song, dance, and cuddling they celebrate the baby's "one-month-old" festival, a thanksgiving for its survival past that frequently fatal period.

But happiness is brief in the life of man. For the shadow of miserable Abbot Fa Hai again darkens their doorway. More accurately, he captures White Snake in a golden alms bowl. It is a scene of spectacular visual beauty. On a slight elevation above White Snake stands a figure the right side of whose face is painted black and the left side a lacquered red. He is a monster of immense strength who works for the depressing abbot, and played by an actor built like a Japanese wrestler. Sword in one hand, with his other he holds a large golden bowl about the diameter of a Volkswagen wheel straight out over White Snake's head, without his arm even trembling for the duration of several arias lasting many minutes. Once under the power of the inverted bowl, White Snake shrinks in defeated terror and is incapable of moving.

Fa Hai buries White Snake under the Lei Fang Pagoda, but this unmerited punishment illuminates Xue Xien's mind. He is left with the baby, for one thing, and with White Snake under the pagoda, his business is shot and he concludes that his enemy is not his wife, the so-called man-eating demon, White Snake, but the feudal leader, Fa Hai, abbot of the monastery. More or less at this point, the deserted husband vanishes from stage and story.

After no one knows how many generations have passed, Green Snake blows up the pagoda and rescues White Snake from underneath it, and they both return to heaven. At this joyous reunion and departure from the troubles of the earth, there is not a thought or mention of her husband, her baby, her medical business, or for that matter anything that has happened. It is just as if nothing had happened at all.

But something really has happened, apart from a display of precision in acting and singing, a production of great verve, costumes that startle the eye and seem filled with light. What is left is very close to a real conviction that when on the Fifth of May you begin feeling uneasy, and you have the impression that you are somehow not who you always assumed you were, it is simply that you are trying to return to your original form, and that you are passing through the memory of the White Snake and her metamorphoses.

It is not only as good an explanation as any for this common feeling, it is also beautiful and somehow satisfying.

Inevitably, plays in Western-style realism, introduced into China only relatively recently in this century, have far less color and excitement. (Our Su Guang attended his first realistic play with us and was surprised that he could find it interesting. But before discussing realism in the theater, I must first return to my walk down the train corridor, for a certain contrast between Western drama and a particularly fantastic encounter on that train.)

He noticed me through the window in his compartment door and rather shyly but with determination came out into the corridor, a small Chinese in his mid-fifties, with wire-rimmed glasses and, like everyone else aboard, looking like he hadn't slept all night, his yellow shirt wrinkled and his eyes gritty. He spoke a careful, correct English, each phrase exhumed from deep in the past.

"You are American, I am thinking."

"That's right."

"I should like to introduce myself."

"Please do. My name is Miller."

"I am Professor Yang of Jiao Tong University, Xian."

The train had slowed to a crawl and through the window beside us we could see a line of a dozen or so peasants crossing a field, both men and women with enormous loads of hay on the ends of their shoulder poles. The weights they carried were so great that they had to move in a kind of forward-falling trot, the poles springing up and down with each step.

The professor noticed my interest in the bearers. "Not at all like the States." He smiled.

"You've been there?"

"Yes, I was sent by my Shanghai firm to work in Connecticut, in a town called Derby."

"I pass through there frequently. What is your field?"

"Physics. Thermodynamics."

"When were you in the States?"

"I went in 1945. In '49, with our Liberation, I wanted to return, but the United States would not permit anyone back to China, especially a trained man. So I went to M.I.T. for another degree. I managed to get out through Canada and France in '52."

I tried to give him a grin of familiarity. "Is it all the fault of the Gang of Four?"

He did not get the joke. "Much of it, no doubt. The country has been stagnating, you know."

"And now?"

Excitement flashed in his eyes. "Oh, this country is on its way up. There is no question about it now."

Roadside, Guangxi Zhuang Autonomous Region

With every new person now I found myself in the position of a child asking its elders where they had been and what they had done during some war or calamity that had happened before he was born.

We talked a little longer, but I found my interest flagging in the familiar litany against the Gang. The truth was that I had passed the point of surprise with the Chinese, who were now merely people, not at all magical, who by their own testimony had got themselves caught in a backward system which might maintain them at a survival level but not really much better than that. It was common to see women in the fields swinging watering scoops suspended from tripods to irrigate crops, precisely as had been done millennia ago. And if the mechanization of the land ever did substitute electric pumps for their labor, what would be done with a mass of displaced laborers?

China, it seemed through the train window, was going to move from crunch to crunch and not necessarily upward at all, and it was almost comical to blame any regime. Quite simply, they had far too many people and were at their wits' end as to how to manage, and more conversation about the Gang was no longer my idea of entertainment.

Back in our own compartment I found Inge puzzling out the Tang poems in Volume I while Su Guang leaned to the gray light from the window with Volume II, his face marvelously placid, filled with an inner joy. Now and then he would glance out the window, his eyes flickering with pleasure from the compact thousand-year-old language in his hand. They will go on forever, I thought, and it is because they have already gone on forever.

So I got up and went down the corridor and brought Professor Yang back. He was very happy to join us.

"Why are you traveling now?"

"We are having a meeting in Shanghai."

"Who is that?"

"The scientific cadres. We are trying to speed up the restructuring of the faculties."

"Because of the Cultural Revolution?"

"Yes. But the Cultural Revolution was very good for us."

"Ah?"

"Oh, yes, very good."

At last! I thought—I am meeting a supporter of the Four. "Then you didn't particularly suffer, personally?"

"Well, they had me cleaning the urinals."

"Part-time or . . . ?"

He caught that joke and laughed. "Oh, no, for two years. I did not teach at all."

"I guess you can understand how hard it is for foreigners to understand. What exactly happened?"

Professor Yang, Xian-Nanjing-Shanghai express

The same curious glaze seemed to pass over his eyes as had afflicted many of the actors, directors, and filmmakers with whom the same question had been discussed. I interrupted the professor. "Is it that you don't quite know for sure whether the Red Guards and all that weren't morally more pure than . . . ?"

"Oh no, no," he quickly corrected, "the Red Guards . . ."

"Who exactly were they?"

He thought a moment. His glasses so needed cleaning that he had to spread his eyes open to see better. "I never knew those people before."

"Well, what'd they do, just come into your lab and . . . ?"

"No, I was teaching that day, a class."

"And they came in?"

"Yes, suddenly there they were."

"How many?"

"Oh . . ." He thought a moment, trying to recall. I was beginning to sound like a policeman investigating a crime, and he a victim who had been slugged and could not clearly piece together his memory. "About twenty of them came in . . ."

"Students?"

"Oh, no. They were not even from Xian."

"They weren't educated people, then?"

"Middle school, possibly, some not even that."

"And they burst into the classroom, and then what?"

"Well, they told everyone to leave."

"And to go where?"

"Wherever they liked."

"And what about you?"

"I also."

"It was just to break up the class?"

"Yes. But later, some of them struggled with me."

"You mean physically?"

"Not in my case."

"What about other faculty?"

"They beat up the rector and some others."

"Why?"

Now behind his grungy glasses, the light from the window flashing on his eyes as well, he seemed further to lose himself in memories that led him to closed doors, pointlessly endless corridors, misunderstood commands, and a terror now healed over in his soul. "I don't believe I recall any more, but there was some reason for the violence, it's hard to say."

"What was your argument with them about?"

"It wasn't quite an argument. It was that they were very angry with me because I—" He broke off, trying to remember.

"Was it that you'd been in the States?"

"Well, possibly it was, yes. There was a terrific hatred of everything foreign." Now he seemed to clear up momentarily. "It was really, I suppose, that they were quite ignorant and did not like or trust anyone like me."

"Had you any ideological position at all?"

"Oh, no, I only wanted to teach physics."

"Maybe that's what they hated—your apolitical mind."

"Except that I am political. It was simply that I was an expert, you see, and they believed that that made me unequal. So that I had to do manual work in order to"—he grinned—"sort of melt into the others."

"So they had you cleaning the toilets."

"For two years, but then they said I could teach again. However, they presented themselves for engineering studies, and they were completely unprepared. Some could barely write and do the simplest mathematics. There were people who'd really never been to school at all."

"So what happened?"

"Well, it just sort of dissolved. The faculty had been either taken off to some detention or else simply ceased to appear. There was nothing for anyone to do any more in the department." He sat there nodding slightly, recalling. "We lost something like twenty years in those ten. If you add up the people who'd have been taught by my students and so on down the line."

"It's now two years since Hua Guofeng took over . . ."

"I know, but it takes a long time to assemble a faculty, to find the right people. We are beginning, though; there are examinations for entrance again, and people are willing to study, and there is respect for teachers again. But it will take a lot of time. We have far fewer university students today in China than in the 1950's, and the population has grown so much since then."

"How many college students are there?"

He counted, staring in the air. "About three hundred thousand."

"In *all* of China?"

"Yes," he said, looking at me stubbornly. "The universities had died."

I would inquire later of others and no figure was over a million students, which most thought was inflated.

"What was your life like then?"

"Well, there were endless parades, you know. At least two or three times a week. All work would stop and everyone had to come to praise or denounce something or someone. Most people tried to avoid parading, but it wasn't easy. The entire city was playing a sort of game, you see, like children." He thought again and, with a perfectly simple, unaccentuated tone, said, "It was anarchy."

"I have asked this question now a number of times and I'd like your answer. You obviously know about our McCarthy period."

"Yes, of course." He smiled with some enjoyment. "I was prevented from leaving America because of that hysteria; especially as a scientist, I could not be allowed back into China."

"Right. But you know, of course, that after a lot of agony, and the destruction of many people—"

He broke in. "Actually, you know, he was trying to destroy the universities too."

"And did a pretty good job here and there. But the point is that ultimately there was a chance to counter him through the press and through minority propaganda which gradually people got to understand. I mean a counterpressure could stop him before he wrecked the United States. Don't you think you people ought to be thinking about some independent organ, some point of appeal, so that you don't repeat that disaster? Because the impulse to destroy the intellect is always there in human beings."

He nodded. Understood perfectly. "I'm sure Hua Guofeng is thinking about that question."

How terrible, I thought—it will never occur to them that the initiative might come from below, from outside the Party. And so the paroxysm will have to come again; it is only by paroxysm, as Mao understood, that the great snake moves at all.

"One more thing," I said. "Could you recall for me—when a person was picked up and sent away, with no real trial or chance for rebuttal of charges, what was the people's reaction? I mean really, deep down."

A physicist accustomed to hard numbers, he smiled as though he were being asked to enter the fudgy world of fantasy. "I don't know, but I can tell you what they'd usually say."

"What?"

"*Mo xu you.*"

"And what does that mean?"

Inge, sitting across from us on the opposite couch, volunteered, "He needn't have committed a crime." And having been raised in Berlin under Hitler, she would add later, when the professor had gone, "It's exactly how they acted in Germany—people just disappeared."

She turned to Su Guang, who all this time had been sunk in his Tang poems until now his eyes were bleary. He handed the volume back to Inge. "Keep it for yourself," she offered.

Bookstore, Xian

"Oh, no," he said firmly.

"Why didn't you let me buy you one, they cost practically nothing."

He turned back to the window. How he wanted the book! But he would never accept it.

And that was true too.

In a little while the chief conductor returned and handed her grammar book back to Inge. Its broken back had been reglued and a new cover had been neatly made for it out of heavy wrapping paper printed all over with birds nesting in the branches of a bamboo. It was beautifully, one might say, affectionately, done.

[1 2]

While we are of course paying our own expenses, we are nevertheless the "guests" of the Friendship Association. That means we must be met by a small delegation in each stopping place and on our first night given a "banquet," hosted by one or two members of the association and sometimes more. The "banquet," we were thankful to discover, required only two, possibly three toasts with thimblefuls of Mao Tai, a potent vodka-like drink of 60 percent alcohol, or their sherry-like, sweetish wine. Actually, the "banquet" was always a delicious but not an immoderate meal spread over many courses, and prepared as it was for our small number of people (sequestered in some private room or corner of the hotel dining room shielded by screens), the food was hot and not lukewarm as it often had to be when served to large numbers of guests.

In Guilin our banquet host is a vice chairman of the city's Revolutionary Council, a good-humored, tightly made fellow in his mid-forties, a full-time political worker who is evidently the Party's man to deal with foreign writers and artists. (Elsewhere, the job was more often held by a writer or artist. In Guangzhou it was a novelist banned for eleven years who was still unable to begin a work. In Hangzhou, it was a writer who had staged shows for the troops at Yanan during the Long March and after, and had known Mao and Zhou. For such as he it would be difficult indeed to utter the least criticism, especially before a foreigner, of the venerated Mao.)

It must be remembered that in the early fall of 1978 we are at the moment immediately before the pustule of Mao-worship would burst open, but there could still be no absolute certainty of that. So his great name was still being spoken in either a neutral or a deeply respectful tone. For a Long March veteran like our host in Hangzhou this attitude would of course come naturally. "Yes," he said, sipping wine, "I used to see Mao almost every day in Yanan. He lived just as we did and he was not the least bit fatter than any of us . . ." And he grinned warmly, lovingly.

The Yanan Museum of the Revolution came back to mind then; a cold and rather desolate building in Soviet mausoleum style, its main exhibit a photomontage running along the walls which showed snapshots of the arrival and life of the Eighth and Fourth Route Armies, and collections of their weapons and utensils; even the white pony Mao used to ride, stuffed but saddled and seemingly ready to go in his glass case, while Mao lies in his crystal crypt in Peking. Ahead of us as we slowly moved along studying the photos were two peasants dressed in clothes so patched as to seem overdone costumes for a naturalistic play. One of them, carrying an equally patched burlap sack on his back, kept clearing his sinuses and wanging great gobs of spit onto the floor, despite the ubiquitous spittoons placed at every conceivable strategic point. Disgusting as it was, one could not help admiring these peasants' evident air of proprietorship—it was their museum.

In any case, it was the likes of the two spitters that had made up the Armies of the Revolution, and it was their faith and resolve that had transformed China. It was also the likes of them, the 90 percent of the people who lived on the land, that any demythologizing of Mao would have ultimately to contend with. For in the few peasant dwellings that we would manage to see there was always a sort of Mao corner where a photo of him, often a color shot from an old newspaper, was tacked to the wall like an icon. If China has no religion, and it has none, Mao was nevertheless as good as any godlike presence and force, and our host's tone in referring to him was appropriate to the departed one's place in cosmology.

Eighth Route Army veteran, Nanniwan

But all this notwithstanding, plus the fact that our host was himself a Party member and an official of the Revolutionary Council, he was easily the most forthcoming and candid of anyone we had so far met when I raised the question of whether any thought was being given to preventing the recurrence of what was now called fascism in China. But even he tensed and giggled (a vocalization which implicitly confirms a fact while apparently, but not necessarily in actuality, making light of its importance; the Chinese giggle is an absolutely invaluable means of healing a breach before it is even visible in social intercourse, while at the same time acknowledging that a breach has in fact occurred). His tension made it clear that indeed my question was not academic at all.

He began answering with light, generalizing strokes. "It is a question we must consider, yes. But ever since the overthrow of the Gang, people are far more vigilant, and they will not permit such excesses to happen again."

"But how will they not permit it? The government controls the press, right?"

"Of course."

I decided, in view of his apparent willingness to discuss the matter, to go all out with him. "And the Party never looks lightly at opposition once it adopts a line, right?"

It was not quite as easy for him to agree to this, but he had courage and he finally nodded, "That is true, yes," and giggled.

"Then for your own welfare isn't it time to think about setting up some institution whose job it would be to hold independent powers of appeal, for example? I mean newspapers or maybe even a new agency within the Party with the right to dissent. I think you are the prisoners of your own decisions and you don't leave yourselves a graceful way out when they don't work. It's a contradiction—you discuss things, you decide, you then demand unity around the decision. And that makes it impossible to put on the brakes if the decision is dumb."

There was a pause. Surprisingly, unlike Chinese and Americans before him on our voyage, this man apparently agreed with my thought. But he seemed, in the pause, to be deciding whether to admit it. Finally he did—"The people are now deliberating about this," he said, and looked directly at me.

"But do you personally believe anything will come of it? I mean, can the Party ever share its authority?"

He thought again, unhappily now, but interested too. And I had the feeling that he had had such discussions before this but that the nerve may not have been touched, and now he was forcing himself to touch it.

"In the early days of the revolution," he said, not quite meeting my gaze, "there was a fine tradition of democracy here. The people —all of them—would vote about everything. They were almost all illiterate, but there were bowls set out and they would drop in black or white beans to vote yes or no on rival issues and candidates. And there is something else."

Su Guang, who was translating, showed a certain excitement in his eyes which was hard to interpret as either surprise at this official being so confessionally candid, or else his own fear of the discussion spilling over its proper limits.

"To be a cadre now has become a profession. It used to be a vocation, work that one did because one felt called to it and to the sacrifices it entailed. A cadre was not the first to be fed but the last, not the first to get living space but the last, and he drank from the bottom of the cup not the top. To be a cadre was not an honor then, it was a walk into the direct line of fire. More than likely, in fact, the people you were trying to help would not understand, at least not all of them, and would distrust you and even hate you. To be a cadre, you see, was not a profession in those times."

We ate. No one spoke. A marvelous sweet-and-sour fish arrived, steaming. Whatever one's feelings about socialism, no one who cared about human beings could exult at the recurrence yet again of the taming of the heart, the splaying out of revolutionary idealism, and this man's puzzlement. But he was far from giving way to despair.

I said, "No country can rely on revolutionary passions forever. Justice has to be institutionalized and put beyond the reach even of the Party itself. You have to protect dissent or you will lock yourselves into your errors. And I want you to understand that in my country that is exactly what we have done from time to time, but one can finally be heard after a lot of waste and a lot of agony."

His comment now was typical of the Chinese. Or was it only the

Maoist in him? He grinned. "But the waste is part of the moving forward. Truth is never a straight line." In short, China had eons behind her, and plenty of time ahead in which to find her proper way.

We ate the fish. I drank more Mao Tai, which Inge would not touch, but Su Guang was on his third and feeling little pain, refusing yet another piece of food and making it vanish at the host's insistence.

I felt that we had narrowed the distance between us. "How'd you get your job? You're not elected, are you?"

"By the Central Committee of the Party, yes."

After four Mao Tais one tends to say anything. "Do the people ever get to vote? I mean, people outside the Party?"

He had not drunk much at all, and so he took time to answer. "Yes, they vote."

"When did they vote last?"

He had to think a while. "About five years ago."

"And when will they vote again?"

He grinned. "I must tell you what I admire most about the Americans."

Su Guang was happy to translate this, and I asked what he admired so about the Americans.

"You always say what is on your minds."

We all laughed.

And then he said, "I would recommend to you a speech by Mao which he delivered in 1962 . . ." It was the speech, widely republished only in the past year or so, in which Mao had warned that if they did not succeed in generating back talk from a feudal people they would end in a kind of fascism.

[1 3]

The paintings on exhibition at the Nanjing artists' center make it easy to imagine what the artist's problem is in China at the present moment. Pictures of happy workers and peasants in heavy black outline, costumes and flesh tones bright and optimistic, alternate with traditional landscapes, somber and rather dark, emphasizing a stylized verticality, the elemental falling water, the mountain and forest.

And indeed the three middle-aged painters escorting us agree there is a tremendous gap between the mute abstractness of traditional art and the poster-like advertising cartoons—no doubt favored by the Party—which are sandwiched in between. "We need a synthesis between them, and we hope a great master will arise who will combine representation and the abstract." At least this can be said aloud, now that the government has changed.

Like the writers, they knew little of Western art, and complained that when the French had sent an exhibition a short while before, it was all landscapes, whereas the Chinese already know everything there is to know about landscape painting. I asked if they were familiar with Van Gogh, thinking that his peasant and village subjects might appeal to them, and indeed they had seen reproductions of his work but never an original that might demonstrate his laying on of layers of oil paint. They agree he might be relevant to their hope of creating a non-naturalistic but still representational style.

The very concept of a personalized art sits uneasily with them, but the pressing guidance of the state was heavy on the painter's hand centuries before the Communists came to power. Indeed, it may be said that most of the world for most of the time has been governed by autocracy of one kind or another, and art is always and inevitably subjected to it. Michelangelo can hardly be said to have had carte blanche from the Pope for his Sistine ceiling, which, needless to say, is filled with images that reinforce the authority of the Christian religion and not the Moslem, Jewish, or Buddhist, and surely not agnosticism or atheism. Art and privacy of inspiration have no very long history together. But the Chinese seem to have a veritable lust for symbolization, probably due to the nature of the language, and more to the point, a fine zeal for symbolic political interpretations of art.

Some years back, one of the painters related, a catalogue had been compiled of paintings to be sold, it was hoped, to foreign buyers in order to raise money to support the Vietnamese resistance to the Americans. Chen Dayu had a painting of a cock in this collection which was carefully examined by the Revolutionary Committee of Shanghai, whose approval was required for the catalogue to be printed.

Explained one of the painters to us now, "They came to the conclusion that the tail of the cock, which pointed to the sky, was too erect, and too high. The cock in China is a fighting bird and this one's eyes were so emphatically large and its claws so very powerful that the figure certainly symbolized the arrogance of aggressive fascism attacking socialism and was basically a rightist picture and was prohibited."

The three painters laughed, as Inge and I did and Su Guang, but one had to wonder how they had maneuvered in that other time. Had they ever been seduced by this hieroglyphic-politics in art? Had it seemed so absurd at the time, when behind it stood an awesome and quite crazy power? Power, after all, makes any absurdity ever so slightly logical. In fact, as they explained, Zhou Enlai had personally selected some of the paintings which the Gang promptly labeled "black," or "returns to the sinister line," and since no one was permitted to know anything about the painters themselves, "a great many innocent folk were convinced of the existence of a nest of counter-revolutionary painters in Nanjing. And none of us was allowed to reply, although there was a tremendous and long-lasting campaign against us in the press."

Now without any discussion we are informed that the three painters present would paint a picture in our honor. A long white sheet of rice paper is produced, and each painter sets out his clump of brushes as well as an elaborate old inkstone. This is a kind of stone, set in a hardwood box, itself often beautifully carved, which absorbs ink very slowly and holds enough of its seepage in a cavity so that a brush can be dipped and wetted. (These stones are precious to painters and old ones in the antique stores bring very high prices.)

The painting is started by one artist, who begins at the bottom, pushing his inked brush against the grain of the soft bristles, making a clump of long half-inch-thick lines running vertically up about a third of the paper. Then with a sharper brush he slashes in what are now obviously pine branches and we have a dense thicket.

Number-two man takes over and with much lighter strokes traces a long curve, which turns out to be a waterfall beginning a little above the midway point of the picture and descending almost to the bottom, the lines splattering off in all directions.

Number-three artist now adds a mountain, which is blocked into the upper right side. Now number two returns and adds a wash of faint pinkish gray to the falling water, and a deeper pink to the pine thicket. Number one moves in again to make the thicket a bit more dense, and three counters with another shot at the waterfall. It's sort of a paint-in, and they are giggling as they add their separate changes, for they have never tried this before. In about twenty minutes we have a good landscape which, if it seems to lack something in feeling, is rather elegantly proportioned and deftly drawn. The most beautiful part of it, however, is the dedicatory column of Chinese characters drawn along one edge and ending in one of the artists' personal name-seals—the others had forgotten to bring theirs along.

The effort, of course, is in part political and prearranged, yet the feeling of the artists is certainly genuine; their curiosity about Western art is too avid to be faked and this gift, they hope, may help open the door to the world a bit wider.

Once again, as we left the gallery, I could not help wondering why public buildings here, as in Russia, had to be so gloomy, so untended, so unloved in conception as well as in their upkeep. We certainly have plenty of ugly public buildings but they at least tend to show some sign of crankiness if not imagination, some awkward or naïve fantasy, or even some truly horrible splurges of bad taste. But in so many post-Liberation public buildings in China there is

Jing Zhenyuan, painter

Left to right: Wu Lingshen, Jing Zhenyuan, Wu Junfa, painters

simply a sort of silence of the eye, as though once the walls were tight against the elements their designers had simply fled the sight of them.

[1 4]

"Why do you worry so much about the future!" Su Guang complains, trying to manage a laugh. "We can't think about the future so much."

I am standing with him at the highest window of one of the two tall towers overlooking the endlessly long Nanjing Bridge. This vast and celebrated construction, with its dozens of arches sunk into the broad Yangtze, all goes to support a road only three lanes wide. "Once you start producing vehicles the traffic jam here is going to reach the Pacific Ocean on one side and Russia on the other," I had said. But at the moment there are only occasional smoking buses lazily making the long crossing, and the usual hodgepodge of bikes, tractors, and hand-drawn carts.

Still, it is an impressive work, perhaps the foremost example of a project built, it is claimed, entirely by Chinese, from the laborers to the engineers and architects. And indeed its main importance, rather than carrying vehicular traffic, is as a railroad bridge, a function which it undoubtedly performs perfectly well on its lower level. It is the Great Wall of Communism, made to last forever, and the look of it is heavy indeed. Especially with the Soviet-style worker-peasant heroic statues of pink cement, which from below seem the size of pyramids, standing at each end. And in a reception hall inside one tower stands a full-length statue of Mao, exactly seven and a half meters high, to commemorate his seventy-fifth birthday. It is shiny white cement or plaster with shoes about the size of filing cabinets, and one of the best examples of the wisdom of the Old Testament's prohibition against making graven images.

But the Yangtze gives it all the grandeur its earthbound design may lack. Like the Mississippi, the river here is broad and sluggish, and its vast sweeping bends are full of mystery. For some reason over Chinese riverine landscapes a haze seems always hanging, as though to invite painters and soothe the eye from the wounds inflicted by man.

On another river, the Li, which threads its way through the spectacular scenery at Guilin, we had the good luck to have arrived before anything at all had been improved. The tourist is floated downriver on covered wooden barges towed by old motorized junks, and wherever on these worn-out boats the eye happens to look there is bound to be a repair done with hammer and nails or a bandage of twisted rope. On an open deck at the bow half a dozen men and a "minority woman" of twenty-five, her young baby

Li River, Guilin

watching her from a nearby impromptu crib, occasionally swing a thirty-foot-long pole to shy the barge off boulders that crop out from the shallow riverbed. This is a Minority Area, the Guangxi Zhuang Autonomous Region, but to the foreign eye the people look little different from the majority Han, except for a slightly flatter and broader face in some individuals.

Even more so here along the open river than when glimpsed from the town, the landscape of Guilin is childlike, the mountains rising almost vertically to rounded tops, each one set apart on a flat plain. Some improbable tenderness seems to emanate from these strangely made mountains, a softness lent them by the river's haze as well as the thirty- to forty-foot-high clumps of bamboo lining the shore, their tops curving in graceful, densely green plumes, like old quill writing pens or the sweeping hat feathers of the Three Musketeers.

This is the scenery of the classical Chinese paintings, which turn out to be far more realistic than one had thought, with their dreamy views of mountain and falling water, the people at their base so small and so robed in silence. The real Guilin is quite as improbably poetic. The junk floating by has rose-colored sails with blue patches the size of a door; another has beige swaths sewed onto a sail of faded rose. The fishermen's rafts are hardly more than two feet wide but twenty long—four or five immense bamboo trunks lashed together. And they sit aboard them on their heels with a woven basket nearby, and bait their lines with a grain of rice—even the fish have Chinese tastes, it seems. And like any child-conceived river, it is shallow but pure and clear, and the fist-sized stones on the bottom gleam in the sun, rolling lazily with the movements of the water. The occasional villages glimpsed along the river are of tan mud, their low and broad roofs seeming snug and inevitable and forever.

And savoring these sights from the sunny yet cool deck of the tourist-filled barge, I can't help smiling at my feelings, which are overwhelmingly nostalgic. The fisherman on his lovely raft who poles himself along will doubtless welcome the coming outboard motor, even if it leaves a pencil-thin trail of spilled oil in the water, and the squatting women beating their wash on the banks can hardly be blamed for staring at magazine pictures of washing machines, as they must have done by now. It is odd to think that we may be living in their future. I stare at them in their motorless silence along their crystal river and hope they manage better than we have, and inevitably think of Thoreau and the intellectual's congenital resistance to change, especially change he has not conceived himself.

If, as has been said, "you can't go farther than China"—it is still possible in the theater for one's sense of human nature's universality to be restored. The Chinese in the theater do not laugh when we would not, and they do laugh when we would. The cultural *information* is quite different, East and West, but what the heart makes of it is similar.

Loyal Hearts is the most celebrated post-Gang of Four play, and the first to reveal some of the details of that period. Its author, Su Shuyang, is in his early thirties and still works in the Traditional Medical Institute as a high-level specialist. Sitting beside us, watching his play, he seemed deeply moved by it, as any new playwright should be. His models, he says, are Chekhov and the Ibsen of the social plays. Clearly, *Loyal Hearts* was fashioned as a blow and a weapon, and its force as a social document seems undeniable; the audience is profoundly moved at the end. That it is also of a realism which is by now pedestrian in the West is not to deny its validity as a play, for the mode fits its subject and the author's intention.

Su Shuyang

The plot concerns old Doctor Fang, who heads a research group that has created 03, a drug for the treatment of heart disease. The government (the Gang) attacks Doctor Fang for catering merely to the big shots of the city, who are alleged to be the main sufferers from heart problems. Should such a charge be allowed to stick, Doctor Fang will be labeled a bourgeois counter-revolutionary and will doubtless suffer professionally as well. He might even be sent off to feed pigs for a few exemplary years. But subjectively, more even than this is involved for the good doctor. A proud, redoubtable old fellow, he has always considered himself a patriot faithful to the revolution. Thus, such charges are an abomination.

As Su Guang's rapid-fire translation poured into my ear, I could not help being discouraged by the sheer childishness of the procedure—imagine even diseases being identified as bourgeois! On second thought, though, a disease like black lung belongs to coal miners, and I recalled a University of Michigan study some years ago which suggested that the psychosomatic illnesses of our middle class collect in the stomach and head, while the worker worries more about injuries to his limbs.

Anyway, in *Loyal Hearts* the accusation has little to do with science, having originated, it now develops, because Premier Zhou had taken a personal interest in this research, publicly complimenting old Doctor Fang on his group's discovery of 03. (Zhou's gesture surprises the audience as much as it would in real life.) Under the conditions of the Gang's regime, Zhou's kiss was apparently a sentence of death. To make matters worse, Zhou (in the play) had talked for a full hour with the members of the research group, and took time at the Fourth National People's Congress to emphasize his belief that heart disease affects all the people, not just bureaucrats, and that its cure and treatment need attention of national scope. Thus the gauntlet is thrown down between the Zhou–old Doctor Fang side, and the Gang, which one ought to remember was nothing less at the time than the government of China, including the aged Mao.

This political conflict is articulated through the old doctor's family and associates. The tone is that of *An Enemy of the People*; the impulsion being preeminently social and moral, there is little or no subjective life expressed and the people have characteristics rather than character. While the dialogue manages to ring in all the main current slogans—"Learning from facts," "Don't forget that all reactionaries will come to a bad end," and so forth—it is also undeniable that below the clichés runs an emotion at least as genuine as the feeling that may underlie any other credo or religious conviction that is expressed in formulas. The current ideological bases may be touched along the way, but there is a loving hand behind it all rather than a mere teaching or disciplinary harshness and it seems to be the love that touches the audience.

It is this, too, which makes a *deus ex machina* at the end seem within the range of emotional reason. The old Doctor Fang perseveres, the perverse or cowardly characters fail to win the day, truth—and China—win out, and the grateful old doctor suggests that his colleagues join him in a letter of thanks to the extremely ill Premier Zhou. As pen touches paper, they hear funeral music—in a howling wind that has begun to blow outside—and Premier Zhou, it turns out, has at that very moment died. The characters weep with grief, and as the funeral music moans in the background, the old doctor faces the audience: "Our beloved premier. You were the good premier of the people. Your loyal heart beat only for the people . . ." and so on. "The Internationale" displaces the funeral music as the curtain descends, and the audience is overcome.

What is interesting here is not the identity of one side or another in this political fight, but the values upheld by the play and its audience. For if Zhou is depicted as determined and fearless, he is also humane, truthful, undogmatic, and warm. So it would seem that nearly half a century of terrible struggle in revolution, famine, and war has not hardened the Chinese to the more liberal civilized ideals—or so this very popular play and its audience would indicate.

But it should be added that the physics professor we met on the long train ride felt that the play, which he had watched on its nationwide telecast, was way over the average man's head and much too sophisticated. "I don't think the peasants had the slightest notion what that play was all about," he said, surprisingly. Surely, I

Arthur Miller between (left) *Cao Yu and* (right) *Su Shuyang, after performance of* Loyal Hearts *at the Peking People's Art Theater*

had thought, the play was clear enough for anyone to understand. Was the gap, then, between country and city, lower and upper grades of education, indeed so incredibly wide?

I was not prepared for a test of my belief that human emotions, at least as expressed on stage, are universal. After the performance of Guo Moruo's play, *Cai Wen Ji*, the seventy-six-year-old director of the Peking People's Art Theater insisted that I must sit down with the cast for a serious discussion of the play. Since the story is medieval and the acting stylized as befits the Traditional Play, I did not feel precisely on home ground with it, and after exchanging greetings with the large cast, I expatiated on the production, magnificent sets and costumes, and the strong and, to me, exotic acting.

Cao Yu, the black-haired director, a restless bantam in his late sixties who cannot sit still or suppress a wisecrack, now commanded silence of his actors so that I could hold forth about the play itself. I had dreaded this. The play, however exotic, had bored me with its relentless repetitiousness. And from what I could detect in the audience's feeling, repetition is repetition in Chinese also. Having praised, and honestly, the acting and production, which could compare with the best anywhere in the world, I hated to have to tell the truth about the play itself, but there seemed to be no alternative.

"Quite candidly," I said, my dread deepening as Cao Yu and the cast held complete silence, along with a line of interested stagehands which had formed behind them, "I assume it comes from my unfamiliarity with your history, but I have to tell you that the play itself I found rather boring."

A startled look instantly flew across all their faces. They were still, of course, in their gorgeous, flowing medieval costumes, and their makeup helped to overemphasize all their expressions, including this one, unfortunately.

Cao Yu, China's great playwright

Cao Yu, eyes wide, said, "Why do you think it bored you, can you tell?" He spoke in English, having spent time in the States in the thirties, when he had learned to adore the work of O'Neill. His two most famous plays, *Sunrise* and *Thunderstorm*, which I had read a day earlier, I found to be impressive, fascinating tragedies of Shanghai life in the decaying China of forty years ago. Indeed, all that gave me the security to launch myself insanely into a criticism of a Chinese play, and one commonly thought a masterwork, was the very evident professionalism Cao Yu showed in the two of his plays I had read.

"I thought," I replied, "that the story was being told four and possibly five separate times in the first hour. The only difference is that new characters repeat it, but they add very little new each time."

Cao Yu let a split second of silence pass. Then, shouting "Hurrah!" he sprang up while the cast burst into applause and nodded deeply toward me, immensely pleased. "Here we are for six months trying to figure out why this play is so boring and he sees it at once and tells us!" A great babble of voices now as the actors with the greatest of pleasure blamed their author in a rapid dialogue whose familiar implications I found myself understanding even before Su Guang could translate them.

"Why don't you stay here for a week and edit it?" Cao Yu proposed, and again the actors applauded, nodding encouragement. As we parted, I thought how odd it was that we should have all been able to understand one another's meaning so easily, and that perhaps only in the theater was this possible. But of course the doctors too, and physicists and other professionals of all kinds, live in fundamentally the same worlds regardless of country or system; it is our histories that differ so vastly and have left us on such varied levels of technological achievement and, hence, strength and tempting weakness.

Of another sort entirely was the anti-Soviet melodrama *Bi An* (Another Hope), in Shanghai. Even in *Loyal Hearts* one could not help noticing the overacting, apparently a common Chinese failing—for it is that in a realistic play. A remark that might call for a smile causes its hearer to laugh; a mild chuckle becomes a guffaw accompanied by deep, appreciative nods. What should be a wave of recognition to an acquaintance turns into a bang of the palm on his back and plenty of ha-ha-ha thrown in. There is also the tendency to start a speech facing right or left to whoever is supposed to be hearing it, ending with the speaker sliding around until he is facing the audience, whose departure the Chinese actor seems to fear is imminent.

It is obviously the operatic tradition, which is venerable and therefore believable, however artificial, while latter-day realism seems to them artificial and unbelievable, enough so that they feel obliged to lapse back into the older form in a pinch. You simply aren't acting if you can't see the audience.

In *Bi An* there is only the shakiest grip even on the realism the play calls for—although the word "realism" hardly describes a story that, apart from its serious political implications, is or sounds like the fantasy of a committee, like those that create some of our own television series. What has to be credited, though, is the mimetic abilities of the Chinese cast, whose imitations of the demeanor and even voices of Russians is both absurdly outrageous and somehow convincing as observation. Perhaps even more amazing is the ballroom dancing by a pair of actors who had never danced or seen anyone else dancing in that fashion. Playing a Russian who is also doing a close-to-the-girl ballroom number in a chic Swiss hotel is for them the parting of several heavy curtains indeed.

Arthur Miller with members of the cast of Bi An *and director Huang Zuolin* (far right), *the Shanghai People's Art Theater*

The director responsible for these triumphs was Huang Zuolin, still another veteran in his mid-seventies. Huang, who hardly speaks above a whisper and moves with deliberation, softly and slowly, spent a year in the thirties in England with his wife, studying theater with Michael St. Denis. He is from a wealthy family—his father was Standard Oil's man in China—and his Mao-Sun jacket, though conventionally cut, is a rich cream color. With his exquisite manners, the nobility of his gestures, and the slow-blooded turnings of his head, he seems the complete Mandarin. He was sent away for three years to feed pigs, study Mao, and confess to his counter-revolutionary dreams.

Huang Zuolin

As it happened, Inge and I were friends of the actress who would come each day to Huang's cell-like room to struggle with him, for she now lives in New York and in fact asked us to look up the old man. We had not appreciated the significance of her suggestion until some intensive days of experience in China; in effect, she had in the sixties been one of the young of the Cultural Revolution who were sent in to shake up their elders until the very last of their bourgeois—or independent—thought had rolled out across the floor and down the drain.

When I realized the situation, I was totally confused. Surely he must resent what she had done to him! But to my question he answered in his measured manner, "Not at all. She was never rude to me, she was merely mistaken, as so many were in those days. As I was, in fact."

And he thought for a moment, and said, "What she did she had to do. It was what you might call her place to do it. Many in her position were rude and cruel and struck people. She was young and full of faith. What can one say? I too was mistaken."

"In what sense?" I asked.

"I thought Zhou supported the idea of people like me being sent away; he must have or it couldn't be happening. I believed that. And so I resolved to try to rid myself of antirevolutionary thoughts, even though I did not know that I had any. And in fact, I didn't have any. It was only in the last few years, in '75 and '76, that we learned there had been a split and that they were trying to destroy us, and the culture, and Zhou Enlai."

I tried to imagine this urbane gentleman feeding pigs and shoveling manure. They must have gotten an extra big kick out of watching him in the mud. I asked him how it was.

He smiled. "I guess the worst of it was seeing my wife, every day for three years, working in a field across a narrow brook and being forbidden ever to talk with her."

"And even then did you think Zhou could have been behind that?"

"One doesn't know what to think after a time."

"Do you think it will ever happen again in China?"

"Yes. I believe so quite definitely. It will happen many times. But perhaps the next time it will be less destructive of what was needed and good."

He knew the past and it was long, and the future was too, it seemed. And once again the thought returned that if there is no tragedy in China, perhaps it is because there is such endless time stretching out behind, and ahead as well.

One day we discussed "Stani" and "Breshit," two schools of theater which Huang, like everyone else, bowed to. But at the same time neither Stanislavsky nor Brecht seemed really to interest them in any definite way. "Our theater, all our art," said Huang in one of his few theoretical musings, "should be, we believe, revolutionary and romantic. I personally believe in the—I find it difficult to say the word in English, but it is translated as . . ." and with some effort he managed to say, "intrinsicalist theater."

"What does that mean?" I asked.

"That we must find the intrinsic reality, the essence of each thing and each relationship and emotion, and to isolate it clearly from what it is not."

I could only nod to what seemed to me the definition of every acting theory I had ever heard of. And anyway, it was not going to matter what the theory was: they were so irreducibly Chinese that the culture would overwhelm any theoretical construct before it became noticeable.

Bi An, the play he had directed, was almost avowedly political propaganda. *Loyal Hearts* was also propaganda, but its lovingness gave it a certain sincerity. In *Bi An* there is little more than high policy, and for that reason it is interesting sociologically, for the audience was without question swept up in its melodrama and seemed to accept its premises.

It starts with a storm the likes of which has not been seen on the American stage since the Belasco stage effects of half a century ago. Palm trees bend in a real wind, branches go flying across the stage behind the scrim, lightning and thunder rip the sky, until despite oneself the thing begins to work on one's mind and one begins to fear.

But it quiets, the scrim rises and the sun comes out and we hear a baritone singing to the sound of a stringed instrument. A woman appears, a Chinese in blackface wearing an elegant turban and a gown with many curving folds in the front, an outfit one associates with tea in one of the better homes of an African capital, but this scene is out in the bush somewhere. Her worried glances to left and right as she cleans off a sort of garden table, preparing it, evidently, for a meal, indicate that the woman is anxious about something.

Now the singer appears, a fine-looking Chinese, also in blackface, wearing a fez and rather an Indian-looking skirt and pretending to play a crude, long-necked two-stringer. One assumes by this time that it is going to be a musical, an old form here which is indistinguishable in its procedures from the older American musicals. But the mood quickly shifts and it is clearly not going to be a musical but something more sinister; a man enters wearing yellow shorts, white knee-length knitted stockings, and a Norfolk jacket and carrying a leather briefcase. He wears a wavy, reddish wig, is hearty, overwhelmingly so, and proceeds after loud greetings to the black couple to remove a bottle of whiskey from the briefcase, referring to the potion as "imperialist wine." He is a Russian and this is Africa; the singer is a faithful follower of a guerrilla leader who is at the moment off fighting somewhere, and the woman is that leader's worried wife.

Along with the whiskey bottle, the Russian has the script of a speech in his briefcase, an address which he and his KGB colleagues have decided the guerrilla leader should deliver at a forthcoming international meeting of the great powers in Geneva. Naturally the speech will praise Soviet help for the African revolution against everybody else's harm.

Watching the Russian in this scene, I could not help recalling how—as I have read—the British were treated in early American plays; they were effete, insensitive, full of themselves, in contrast to the Americans, who might be countrified and unlettered but in their homespun crudeness still shone with moral beauty in comparison. And besides, they always outwitted the more elegant foreigners.

There is no need to explore the plot beyond its main thrust; the KGB decides to assassinate the guerrilla leader because, against their orders, he has decided to assert his and his country's independence in a speech of his own he intends to deliver in Geneva, a slap in the Russian face. This information is inadvertently given the Russians by the guerrilla leader's faithful follower, who opened the play with his song, and who, like most faithful followers, is a bit stupid but makes up for it with his sentimental worship of the leader and later with his remorse for having helped bring him to grief.

It is official art, a poster of a play, but it is not without some touches of observation and strong acting where the script momentarily allows. The KGB chief, for example, out-Russians any Russian ever seen on this earth; a Chinese with immense shoulders, a baritone voice, big hands, a set-shaking laugh—and of course wraparound sunglasses which he never, never removes. (These are the same sunglasses the American imperialists always wore when much the same kind of play was written about the CIA.) He is terrifying when he calls in the manager of the Geneva hotel where he has his dark paneled office and "offers" to buy the hotel then and there so that he and his cohorts can be free to murder the guerrilla leader in his room without interference.

There is an immensely funny moment in the opening scene when the KGB man in his knitted socks and Norfolk jacket and red wig takes out his whiskey bottle and, with the palm trees of subtropical Africa waving over the guerrilla leader's mud hut, asks if there is any ice. The character's stupidity is right out of Gogol, in fact.

In this scene too, a pheasant suddenly flies up from the shrubbery backstage, guided by an easily visible wire, a delightful effect for the audience, topped only when the bird once again takes off across the sky from the tree in which it landed, on another wire, naturally.

In Switzerland, there is also a female spy, acted of course by a Chinese successfully made up to look European. When she enters wearing a tight beige skirt and revealing blouse, wolf whistles fill the air from the Communist audience, a refreshing sound, it being so patently unrehearsed. At that moment one had to wonder at what level of seriousness the whole play was being received. On the other hand, Chinese audiences are notoriously relaxed, continuing to talk while the play proceeds—especially at the opera—and might well whistle at one moment and at the next be fairly serious, the sublime and ridiculous again cheek by jowl.

One could not help smiling when a young Swiss waitress, beaming with good health and apparently well paid, her uniform a lovely sky-blue skirt and jacket, addressed an old porter (a noble revolutionary immigrant Turk with reddish curls turning up under the borders of his fez, and a Swiss pipe curving out under his guards mustache), telling him, apropos of not very much, that "in China women have more rights." It was not possible to interpret the silence that greeted this line, which, considering what prosperous happiness the speaker seemed to be enjoying, must have been somewhat mystifying.

Like the delightfully naïve flight of the pheasant in Scene 1, a jet plane is seen through the tall airport windows in Geneva coming in for a landing, a truly fantastic effect. It reminded me that Stanislavsky, when he came to New York, saw fit to write a letter to Belasco, then at the height of his powers, saying that in his, Belasco's, shows the Russians saw the realization of what they were attempting to achieve. Belasco's stage effects included a Childs Restaurant—it was then a famous chain—complete with the big window facing Broadway through which crowds could be seen passing by, big-bladed fans turning slowly overhead, waitresses in standard Childs black uniforms, customers eating real food at white marble tables—and flies! Or at least the customers' efforts to swat them. The flies were the talk of New York. Belasco was also responsible, in his other, more romantic vein, for a scene in which the hero is about to be shot by an execution squad of U.S. troops in the West, when the heroine suddenly throws an American flag over him and challenges the soldiers to fire *now*, paralyzing them probably for the remainder of their lives.

So the likes of *Bi An* is not without precedent in the history of the theater, but I would wager that as a type it will not last very long once foreign plays of sophistication move onto the Chinese stage, as they inevitably will. For the time being, however, *Bi An* provides excitement and moral reassurance, as well as an outlet for the widespread feelings of betrayal and anger with the Russians. And when the *Bi Ans* vanish, there will be people who will miss their straightforward morality and head-on melodrama. Scenes, for example, like the one when the KGB subchief, among whose sinister traits is his slick ballroom dancing, is trying to decide—this "revolutionary"!—whether to take his secretary off for a weekend in Paris or Egypt. Or perhaps the great moment at the end of the play when the guerrilla chief lies in a Swiss hospital bed dying of bullet wounds. His faithful follower arrives to beg his pardon for having inadvertently betrayed him and—hardly able to open his eyes a moment before—the chief struggles to a sitting position, spreads out his arms, and sings for several minutes at the top of his voice before dropping back on the pillow to die. The time will come, no doubt, when theatergoers will regret the passing of such stirring highlights.

Certainly our local interpreter, a woman of manic energy who insisted on whispering her imaginative translations into Inge's ear while Su Guang kept me up to the minute, was an excited participant in the action. When a curtain fell on a scene she would exclaim, "The next one is a very tense one, yes!" Of an angry actress she whispered, "She feels very indignant in her chest, yes!" which along with "splitting their phrem" kept the flow of her language lively and spiced the play's dialogue. At one point a boat is seen on the Swiss lake at the back of the set. "It's a junk!" she cried out. When the boat started to move, she pointed to be sure that Inge noticed, and urgently whispered, "It's a junk moving, yes!" According to her, "People are waiting for their lugrage," and one of the characters in the play "has bought a shoespate to clean his teeth, yes." But in the end her valor and sheer determination to go on admiring everything she laid eyes on, in or out of the theater, could only overwhelm us with a feeling of helplessness and finally admiration. Whether riding in the car or walking in the streets, she was constantly pumping Inge for the right English word or phrase, of which she made instant note, and if her persistence was irritating from time to time, it was also an attestation of her will to perfect her abilities, and that will was fearsome. She was also the only one who may have tried to mislead us, claiming that a certain woman we visited in a three-room housing project apartment was a typical tenant, when in fact that much space is most often crowded into by three families rather than one. Likewise, in a Shanghai street one day she alone grew quite anxious and was on the verge of insisting that Inge definitely not photograph a string of decrepit but fascinating old houses, pointing out a brand-new apartment house right around the corner, which, however, was indistinguishable from anything in the Bronx. She was, in a phrase, the Mother of Us All, Chinese version, and her passionate vitality indicated beyond doubt that there must be others out there holding the country together.

[1 6]

After nearly a month in China spent talking with people whose lives and careers were harshly disrupted by the upheavals of the past twelve years, I find myself far less diverted by what at first had seemed a veil of exoticism through which our relations with them were filtered. It is not their being Chinese which creates the air of soft indirection between us, their sometimes bewildering etiquette to the contrary notwithstanding, but their suffering a deeply shocking disorientation about their own past and about certain specific fundamentals of their Marxist-Maoist creed.

It is as though they had still not recovered from a trauma whose meaning was unclear, and indeed many of them, like the director Huang Zuolin, would volunteer that it would be a long time before people understood what had happened to them between 1966 and 1978. What had begun as a political-philosophical conflict was now a spiritual-psychological one whose dimensions not only foreigners found it hard to grasp. I may as well admit that in their company it frequently crossed my mind that they were like survivors of a cult whose leadership had been exposed and stripped of spiritual authority. They may now have been freed of irrational threats and discipline but they were also no longer loved and cared about to the point of violence. Even worse, perhaps, they had learned to distrust their own judgment of reality.

One had to sense a certain consistent dourness among those we met, an unrelieved mournfulness beneath their attempts at optimism, and it was not the sadness of the tragic vision but of spiritual confusion with its threat of inner chaos and defeat.

In Shanghai one morning director Huang brought the writer-actress, Huang Zongying to our room. She is a woman now in her fifties who had spent three years in a cadre camp in order to remold her mind. She had the purposeful manner of a professional, an ironic smile, and a glint of wit in her eye from time to time, but again, there was a darkness moving in her, a weight of the unsaid or perhaps the unsayable.

Her husband, Zhao Dan, a notable actor and veteran of forty

Huang Zongying, actress

years in the profession, had been picked up and detained for five years and three months. I asked, "Was there some specific reason given for taking him away?"

She drew a deep breath and sighed, staring past me toward some scene in her memory, and as with Huang Zuolin and so many others, the very specificity of the question was what she seemed to find it hard to deal with. For as I knew by now, people had not necessarily been charged; they could be pressured into departing for camp or simply dragged away or even invited to come. And some would volunteer, as, it turned out, she had done. And now—now that she was being asked by a foreigner for some rational justification for her husband's losing over five years of his precious life, it seemed beyond her to explain it in any concrete way. Yet she, like Huang, had obviously cheered on the Cultural Revolution at some point. There is nothing as disturbing to Marxist rationalism as the surreal and there has been no more surrealistic period in any country's recent history than the Cultural Revolution in China.

"I am trying to understand," I said, "and it would make it easier if you wouldn't mind giving some specifics. Could you?"

"They accused my husband of having done something back in the thirties. He had been imprisoned then."

"By the Guo Mindang, I assume."

"Yes. But you see the Guo Mindang killed a great many suspected radicals, so if someone was released by them it was difficult for that person."

"You mean he would be suspected of having made a deal with the Guo Mindang."

"That's correct."

"So thirty or so years later they accuse him of collaborating with the Guo Mindang?"

It was not the three-decade delay in the accusation, however, that appeared odd to her. "Yes," she replied, explaining, "of course I can't say that I knew for a fact he was innocent—I hadn't met him yet in the thirties—but I believed in my heart that he was not a reactionary. I would have seen *some* sign of it and there never was any."

But the concept of political crime, of believing wrongly and thus meriting imprisonment, remained unquestioned in her. I could only note this; to remark on it was fruitless, I saw. "So for you there is no explanation even now for why they arrested him."

Her expression had become abstracted. I cannot pretend to know why, only that I am sure the same kind of thinning out of *presence* had occurred with many others we had talked to. She was laboring, it seemed, with something dreamy and shapeless within. At the moment it appeared to me that the very concept of considering her husband's case so separately from anyone else's seemed odd to her; the idea of his being innocent in the discrete, quasi-legal sense which I was implying was not a customary thought to her. Legal guilt and innocence was not an issue for them, of that I am certain. Glancing at the imperturbably dignified posture of Huang Zuolin seated beside her, I wondered if he, a quarter of a century older than she and with experience in Europe, had totally forgotten the notion of a written legal code, if only as a point of reference now, a spiritual compass heading. But he showed no sign of any such awareness.

Was their confusion the result simply of accepting the principle of political crime and guilt, while at the same time knowing that so many, including themselves, had suffered punishment and even death at the hands of zealots unworthy of judging them—zealots, moreover, with whom they had sympathized?

The unspoken, perhaps the unspeakable, question hanging in the air was about their alienation. Not from socialism, which no one questioned, but alienation from the process that had both destroyed great hunks of their lives and, as was now admitted, set back their country for one or two decades. And that process, however it might be concealed by words, was that there was no orderly or systematic appeal from the principle of the Party's monopoly over every living thing.

Thus, director Huang's seemingly idle remark that the Cultural Revolution would recur many times in the future took on new meaning. It was not an aberration at all, but the means by which China would move into history, paroxysm by paroxysm, periodically swelling with immensely successful enterprise, the "Correct Line," the health of a thriving nation—all of which, however, would secrete subtle poisons into her blood, specifically the elitism of her irreconcilable and yet irrepressible history. And the top dogs would again have to be humbled and the poisons of privilege vomited up yet again, until once more she was cleansed and a new period of peaceful work might for a time begin. And it would all have to happen in the streets, by the helter-skelter of wild bands breaking into institutions and throwing the files out the windows and burning the books and shooting from rooftops, and the laughter and the mistaken killings and arrests. I had asked director Huang how it had happened that they had let him go, after so many years as their prisoner. He raised his eyebrows, narrowed his eyes, and a tiny, discreet smile played across his lips. "They came one day and said that I was innocent." Then he laughed faintly.

And as we sat there with the two of them in our hotel room Rewi Alley's face floated across my mind. He had been on the scene this half century, the Virgil who had held the lighted lamp before generations of foreigners, including Edgar Snow, through the Hells and the Paradise of China, and I had heard the contradiction—one facet of its complications—inadvertently from his lips. Over tea and cookies one evening in his Peking apartment I had ventured the notion of an orderly system to replace scoundrels in office, and he of course had seen the West's parliamentary system behind my words and said, with sharp and unconcealed disgust, "And they replace one scoundrel with another, with somebody worse, in fact. No, no," he said protectively, "they'll be having none of that here."

And yet later in another context, perhaps before he could think— "Yes, of course, what's so hard for people to understand is that the United States is a democracy, for Christ's sake!" Nor did he apparently mean to include Britain's class system, New Zealand his homeland, corrupted now by a streak of bad politics, or any other land but America. Perhaps, I thought, he had understood Watergate.

Rewi Alley

And he, like Huang, had also absorbed the long view, proudly saying, "Mao had warned them, the Cultural Revolution hotheads, that they should argue but not fight, and that if any violence was done it would be paid for later. And now"—two to ten years after the commission of crimes—"they're hauling them in!" He was grinning happily, and his eyes flashed a joy of vengeance. "And some are in the clink already. Providing!"—he held up his index finger— "they committed violence against people."

So for him too there need be no time limit on retribution, any more than for the actress-writer before me, or for Huang Zuolin, motionless and listening beside her now. China was long and long and long in both directions. But had Alley not, I wondered, been enthusiastic about the coming of the Cultural Revolution, and was he feeling remorse, regret, or nothing? "There were things I wanted to write in '70," he had said cryptically, "but they'd have backed me out a window if I had." And yet, it seemed, this too was not absolutely violative of the rules of Chinese reality in this revolutionary period.

Or was I entirely missing the point and there were not to be any rules at all, ever? There was talk in the press of a drive to establish "socialist legality," but there was no sense of urgency about it. Did they already know that real law, binding on the authorities as well as the people, inevitably meant a cell of independence beyond the reach of the Party and ultimately an intolerable affront to its Leninist power monopoly?

Suddenly, the actress—as though subliminally sensing my obsession with the mystery of their lives—said, "He was not afraid in that other time."

"Your husband?"

"Yes."

"You mean when the Guo Mindang arrested him."

She nodded. "But this time we were afraid."

"Why? Or don't you know?" I pressed on.

She shrugged and shook her head. Surely the legendary ferocity of the Guo Mindang political police was fearsome enough. Or was it simply that they had been clearly alienated from the old Guo Mindang bourgeois society and it was possible to face torture or death at its hands because one knew one was right, that one had honorably borne one's share of history, that one had counted for something in a righteous fight.

But to have been arrested and punished by Red Guards who represented Mao himself, the very oracle of history and the soul of righteousness—this indeed must have been terrifying. For, condemned by the revolution, one was condemned by one's own conscience and one had sinned against the whole world.

This was when Huang, in his barely audible voice, said to me, "We are still trying to understand those years, you see."

The actress-writer looked distracted now, but seemed to suppress something that she had begun to say. (What stories, novels, epics we were stumbling through here! I certainly would never know the whole complex tale but would one of their writers ever tell it, unvarnished and in all its contradictions? She, for example, had volunteered for cadre camp after her husband's arrest and had evidently been kept there for over three years— Had she been a militant? Perhaps one of those who had taunted this Mandarin-type sitting beside her now?)

"Why did you volunteer for the camp, Huang Zongying," I asked her, "to join your husband?"

"Oh, no. I wanted to re-educate myself."

"What was that like, the feeling? Was it the desire to be part of the people, to get rid of any distinction?"

"Yes, something like that," she replied.

There was no spontaneity of recollection she would share. Was it simply that they were on the verge of having to blame Mao for damaging China and feared to, or simply could not, bring themselves to condemn him? For no outsider could know what contrasts Mao brought to their minds.

The dead starved bodies that used to be picked off the streets of Shanghai every morning, the children that had had to be drowned or sold because there was no food for them, the kowtowing to any foreign pipsqueak simply because he was foreign and hence superior, and the filth of China's cities, the rot, the sexual and economic enslavement of women and young girls. What all these things were not, was Mao.

And so to sit now in Shanghai with a foreigner and even so much as imply that Mao had harmed the revolution . . . had perhaps even brought it to the indignity of its manipulation by a vain and spoiled woman . . .

"Could it all happen again, do you think?" I asked her. I knew already that Huang serenely believed it would probably recur.

"I am not a prophet," she said, "but I do not believe we would allow ourselves to be taken in that way again."

"Why, are you more skeptical now?"

The word "skeptical" caused a three-way discussion between them and Su Guang, who finally cleared up its meaning for them. And Huang Zongying turned back to me and replied cautiously, "We are all a mixture of optimism and skepticism."

"That's true, yes," I could only agree. "But I'm wondering if you are a little closer to our Western misgivings about power now."

Equating China in any direct way with the West was out of bounds, obviously, and resistance to the notion sprang onto all their faces, including Su Guang's.

Huang now seemed, for the first time, actively and personally curious. "What sort of misgivings do you mean?" And the actress-writer and Su Guang were no longer having a mere discussion but were clearly manning a defense.

"Well, to oversimplify, misgivings about the ability of men in government really to solve problems that government traditionally claimed it could solve."

"You mean in America?" the old man asked with surprise.

"Yes, America, Europe . . . and in the Soviet Union."

With the last they avidly agreed. But they were not about to give up on America.

"People are disillusioned," I continued, thinking that we could now join hands on this, "because, for one thing, material wealth has not brought them the happiness they thought it would."

The Bund, Shanghai

Now there was open surprise and mystification in their eyes at this cliché. And their deep isolation, which their reaction implied, threatened any hope I had of a common understanding with them. And so I altered the attack:

"I mean that people, many of them, everywhere" (just as here, I would add in a moment, I thought) "no longer know why they're alive, they can't find any meaning in existence." This seemed to me a fair description of what they themselves appeared to be feeling.

But instead of even nominal agreement, a genuine mystification spread over their faces. Even Su Guang, who never interjected his own questions or opinions, could not desist, he was so bewildered.

"What do you mean?" he protested, almost as though I had betrayed him after we had become so close. "Why hasn't material wealth brought them happiness?"

I realized I was talking to a man who did not have access to a bathtub and the absurdity of what I had to say was suddenly stunning. "You've got to try to understand, Su, that for a lot of people in the U.S. there are really no longer any unfulfilled material needs. For millions there is still not enough of most things, but for probably the majority there is materially very little more they really require. And so the question rises—why does one live? What is life for, once there is a surplus like that?"

The words were hardly out of my mouth when I regretted them.

The three Chinese were incredulous—how could one doubt what the meaning of life was! Their country was at war, in effect, and so close to the edge of its resources that its very survival was always at the edge of consciousness; for one thing, should they grow weak enough the Russians would certainly move against them—a not at all theoretical consideration in their minds.

"And you?" Huang asked, an amazed look on his face.

"What about me?"

Su Guang could not help speaking up. "Don't *you* know the meaning of life?"

I felt embarrassed, not by the question so much as by my foolishness in thinking we could all trot along side by side harnessed in the West's most worn-out assumptions. "Well, I suppose for me it has to do with trying to oppose injustice."

"Yes! That is it for us too!" Su strongly agreed, immensely relieved that we could be friends again.

Of course my simplification had changed the subject, but it was hopeless to try to straighten us all out. Anyway, Su was going on:

"The reason we live is to build up our country," an accomplishment so distant in time, I saw, that there was simply no reality in thinking beyond it. They were, in this, thoroughly American, as Americans had been in the long ago. To his declaration Huang and the actress nodded in avid agreement, and they were also relieved, like people who at last had swum ashore. "That is the meaning of life, isn't it?" Su concluded.

I was exhausted now and I nodded, indicating that it was indeed.

Later, standing alone at the tenth-floor window overlooking Shanghai's one-time foreign concession with its tall British- and French-built hotels, like ours in the international style of the twenties, I stared down at a street of once-elegant shops, now dismally empty, that had carried some of the most elegant clothes and expensive luggage and jewelry in the world. The drizzle may have helped, but in its snug architectural tone the quarter was reminiscent of London's Mayfair around the Dorchester Hotel and cosseting Mount Street, and it was not at all difficult to imagine the Rolls and Bentleys and Delahayes driving up and the golden lasses stepping out to join for luncheon the cheery young gentlemen through whose hands the cargoes in the harbor passed and left behind percentages.

Street scene, Shanghai

More difficult was to imagine corpses lying alongside these buildings, thrown into trucks each morning by the hundreds and thousands—if one added in the other cities of China. And it was not far away from this bastion of the upper and middle classes that a rich peasant's handsome son named Mao had attended the first clandestine meeting of the Communist Party of China in 1921.

Soon we would sit down for lunch with octogenarian Talitha Gerlach, who would glance out this window and laugh, saying, "It's all a miracle! No one is starving in China! It is still an unbelievable fact to me!" She had come in the twenties for the YMCA, one of a troupe of American religious, a handful of whom had turned radical with the Chinese and had been allowed to remain. And like the other Americans, but altogether unlike the Chinese, she could not bring herself to an even implicit rejection of the past decade's insanities. For her it was more than enough that the streets were swept, that the young Chinese were literate, that epidemic disease was no more, and the stink was gone. And like the Chinese back home who would be amazed by Inge's pictures of lakes and orderly parks and public places, the miracle was that these were no longer mounded up with the garbage of decades as they had once been. I was now staring down at the Shanghai where Rewi Alley, over thirty-five years ago, had been a factory inspector and had seen chattel slaves working at textile machines, women and children living the lives of scavenging rats, in a city whose real governors were its gangster chiefs, recollections that forbade him despair now. Likewise Talitha Gerlach, who still traipsed around Shanghai cheerfully tending to her social work and trying to make her eighty-year-old self useful. The crashing waves of the Cultural Revolution had passed far above her head up there on the surface, just as they had hardly reached down to the depths where the average peasant had risen with the morning and gone to bed at night in his immemorial discipline that fed the frenzied youth.

Talitha Gerlach

"The artists, writers, theater folk—they're the ones who got it in the neck," Rewi Alley had told us.* Not that he was trying to underestimate the damage done outside the arts. Sitting like a Buddha in his wide armchair, he had grinned rather defensively, it seemed to me, even when with great and lighthearted admiration he assured us, "Hua Guofeng did the thing beautifully, you know. He moved in on them [on the Gang of Four, arresting them all] and did it deftly, without a drop of blood. Nip," and he scissored his two fingers, cutting their connection with power. Rewi had just celebrated his eightieth birthday and had been feted in high places and had the right to feel great about a well-fought life. The little Chinese orphans he had adopted years and years ago were all solid citizens now.

But a month later, as I stared down at the drizzle falling on

* William Hinton, in *Hundred Day War*, his firsthand description of the Cultural Revolution in Qinghua University, where it all began, writes: "Only a minority were consistently active as rebels or as loyalists. The bulk of the campus population of 40,000 tended to be drawn in during the high tides of the movement, only to fall into apathy . . . as the tides ebbed. Toward the end, when factionalism developed to the point of armed struggle, only a few hundred people actually took part. Thousands left the area altogether . . . other thousands stayed home in the family quarters and set up patrols to keep factional 'fanatics' out."

Shanghai, the grace notes of bravado I had thought I heard in Rewi's laughter returned to mind with added importance. He had to have known then that Mao's edifice was tilting over. The China he had devoted a life to might change unrecognizably in these swift new currents. And I recalled more clearly now his air of facing down some inner uncertainty, no different from the looks on the faces of the Chinese we had subsequently met. The truth was that Maoist-Marxism, the science of reality, had left them stunned in a nightmare, a directionless space. All that was sure was that absolutely anything was possible.

I sought an analogue in America to this crisis, which was as spiritual as it was practical and political. Perhaps there had been a moment of such drift and fear when Lincoln was shot and his enemies were exulting and no leader had appeared who stood above his boot tops. But that picture lacks one immense Chinese element—with Lincoln dead, Americans had no reason to overturn their faith in him and revise their attitudes in a 180-degree turn. The last Chinese decade, it was now being said, was fascist, the equivalent of a pastor in his coffin being discovered to have cloven hoofs.

But it was far worse even than that. For Mao had not only wielded power, he had also been good and he had prophesied that the last would be first in China and after China in the whole world by her example. If in his first ten years he had thrown the net of Soviet methodology over China, he had also, astonishingly at the time, revolted against even them, his early mentors, for nothing was to be held sacred except the people. He had not merely led the Chinese people, he had redeemed them before themselves and history. Contemptible, bought and sold by foreigners like field animals —in the United States only Orientals had ever been specifically excluded by law—Mao had lifted them up and the chief men of the world had come before him and bowed down. Mao was a poet, a wit, and an ironist besides, and who could doubt his love for the Chinese people?

If one could even for an instant enter into the Chinese condition, the marvel of it was that they dared now to turn upon this godhead at all, that they had so quickly, less than two years since his death, ceased trying to justify what they knew he had failed in. The Germans after Hitler had not managed such detachment and, actually, such an assumption of responsibility, nor had the Russians after Stalin.

But the question remained whether this calamitous shaking of their deepest beliefs could really be taken to heart, whether the techniques of democracy, a word suddenly on so many lips, were indeed within their grasp.

Certain things had surely been learned, among them that under socialism not less than capitalism the human being was unsafe without the protection of his rights by law, and law that the state too was obliged to obey. Was it conceivable a Communist Party would willingly share its monopoly of power even with its own judiciary? Was such a sharing of power not the opening for that anathema, a second, opposition party?

China had been, for an indeterminate number of years, in a state of anarchy, from time to time beyond the control of Mao himself. He used to say that he did not know how to make socialism because it had never been done in China, but that he was going to try, and he had been the Great Improviser, and now it appeared that the largest population in the world had been governed at times like a children's summer camp: the loudest mouths and the purest of the pure and the reddest of the Red had taken turns whipping the people on with slogan and gun, and a generation had been wasted in detention or by murder or driven to suicide.

And after thirty years and with a soaring population—encouraged by Mao until he had been forced to advocate birth control—doubling to nearly a billion, China was on the dire edge of food crisis again if Hinton was right, unless a real mechanization of agriculture took place rather than the present cosmetic one. But what happens then to the displaced millions? The answer given is new industry in the countryside. We shall see.

Despite the charm of her old operas, China after thirty years is a cultural desert. For the artist there, it is a difficult, impossibly distorting life, but, more important, the absence of any independent cultural response to reality deprives the people of direction, of the self-image that man requires in order to orient his sense of himself. Will the Party now resolve to free the artist so that China may confront herself before rather than after calamity? This answer also is unknown, but surely the freeing of art opens the way to unorthodoxy and once again requires a political party willing to give away part of its power.

All the liberal attitudes that Western Marxists and often liberals as well taught themselves to despise are now written across the posters on Chang An Avenue. The Chinese have discovered the eighteenth century and the victorious revolutions against feudalism, whose first business was the writing of laws demarcating the powers of government and governed. That a peasant or worker sits in the seat of the mighty is no guarantee that he will not oppress peasants and workers. The ultimate contradiction, thought impossible, came to pass: the workers' and peasants' state oppressed the workers and peasants. Nothing is safe from man and everything is up for grabs where there is no law.

Leaping upward out of China now are the rockets and flares and signs and signals of every description which the world and the Chinese themselves will be reading for a long time to come. And one of these is the question of how it happened that this "fascist" government managed to so charm correspondent after correspondent into a kind of reportage which left no impression of the real magnitude of the Chinese disaster. Was it that the Chinese are so poor and so hard-working that even their self-destructiveness must be mitigated in the writing? At least this is no longer the prevailing view within China; nor will the word "left" automatically arouse respect any more, not when it can mask a power-hungry and empty-headed killer of the dream.

China surprised us in a hundred ways, perhaps most of all by her pervasive beauty. There is an instinct for aesthetic harmony among the Chinese, even in the thoughtless way a woman will arrange a handful of leeks she is washing by a brook, setting them down in a fan shape. The Chinese child is a triumph of humanity, and in the aged there is a sort of dignity that can come only from social respect and a decent tradition. There is also a certain rightness of proportion, a native taste in objects held in the hand. And a poetic tradition inconceivable in the West—where else in the world is a leader's calligraphy of importance, and where could it evoke pride that it is elegant? Indeed, the use of imagery in political discourse threatens to turn China into a fairyland for the unwary foreigner. And what people so profoundly understands food?

Kindergarten, Shanghai

But none of these charms can any longer distract the Chinese from their dilemma. It is repeated and it seems to come from the heart—their feudal heritage still holds them. So much so that the very people who say so are at the next moment caught in it again, like the vice chairman of the Revolutionary Committee of Guilin, who emphatically agreed when I asked if their problem was not to guarantee the people's right to at least reply to government, rather than passively to await the announcement of new lines and tactics.

"Oh, yes," he had replied, "it is exactly so. But we understand very well that when you address the masses you have to repeat the same thing three or four different ways before they understand you. You must be patient with them."

I had thought the translation was at fault, and corrected him. "I meant the opposite—the right of the masses to speak up to government, not the government to the masses."

He was embarrassed, I thought, but that he was seemed encouraging. "Yes, of course," he said, evidently recognizing that his reaction had been as feudal as others he had been lamenting a moment earlier.

"There is an underground literature everywhere in the country," Hinton had said, but when I asked if its content was democratic he could not say and, knowing China, would not theorize. But no history dies quickly, as was clear from the gentlemanly old director Huang Zuolin's view of art. We had been discussing his, and his wife's, incarceration and how impossible it had been for any individual to resist, to speak out against that waste of talented people which was taking place across China. And somehow the conversation had made a quick turn to aesthetics.

"Our art must be revolutionary and romantic," he had said. And that, I knew, was another way of demanding, even yet again, an art that would generate popular support for whatever the Party's line was at the moment, an art whose "romantic" nature meant that it would not stand as witness to reality and life but project an "ideal" of what should and would be someday. Despite his and his country's needless sufferings, was a decent old man inadvertently prepared to cut the country off from those images of reality which art can most vividly create, and which at their profound best toughen a nation's spirit against self-pity and self-delusion and may, as has happened, cry up warnings of calamity in good time? Worse yet, this theory of art was devised to serve Power, but in effect it was also Chinese tradition that the captive imperial artist help justify to the people the works and ways of Power.

Simply by acting as a witness to reality, a healthy art would test the Party's monopoly on truth.

We had happened totally by accident to arrive in China at the moment when, it would seem, all Romance was over and the time had arrived to face hard facts. Mao had apparently acted out his own prediction of 1962 and, failing to democratize China, had sunk into a kind of tyranny himself. But, as with Inge's photographs— taken with no such idea in mind—the Chinese past inevitably overwhelms even what the camera sees. And Mao is the past now and in true Chinese fashion the further away he is carried by time the larger he will loom in the mind. Already one could not help grinning at the irony of his having invented and preached a kind of endless overthrowing, a ceaseless renewal, a perpetual revolution— even against himself. And now at last in death his preachment had rooted itself in the people, paradoxically in the very movement to diminish him, a step they had to take if they were ever to put behind them the age-old obedience to masters. The docility, the toadying to the powerful which he so hated in them, filled a 1962 address to the Party's vital core, the cadres, many of whom were themselves the barely disguised targets of his thrust: "Some bad people, some bad elements who have infiltrated into our ranks, and some degenerate elements ride on the backs of the people, piss and shit on them, behaving in a vicious and unrestrained way, and seriously violate laws and discipline." Presumably, the people had stood still for this contempt from on high.

It is against such a history that the post-Mao search for democratized institutions augurs the ultimate victory of that paradoxical man, for the people may now be making him unnecessary to their progress. And there indeed would be an irony, for in that case they would be needing him forever.

Peking. Corner tower, wall, and moat surrounding the Old Palace, as the former Imperial Palace is now called. It was also called the Purple Forbidden City; the color purple was symbolically attributed to the North Star and was used to show that the Imperial City was a cosmic center.

Great drums and gongs
hung on spiked frames
sounding to perfect rule and rote
about the king's calm crescent moat.

Tone unto tone, of drum and gong.

About the king's calm crescent moat
the blind musicians beat lizard skin
as the time weaves out and in.

—From *The Book of Songs* (Chou dynasty),
translated by Ezra Pound

(*opposite, top*) Peking. Inside the former Imperial Palace; partial view of the Palace of Peace and Longevity.

(*bottom*) Detail, nine-dragon screen in polychrome glazed tiles, near the Gate of Imperial Supremacy. This palace was first built in 1689, then embellished and refitted from 1772 to 1776 by Qing Emperor Qian Long, who hoped to retire here after his abdication.

(*above*) Peking. Imperial Palace: gilded bronze vessels in front of the Hall of Supreme Harmony. The hall was used for ceremonies marking great occasions: the winter solstice, the New Year, the emperor's birthday, the publication of the list of successful candidates in the imperial examinations, the nomination of generals at the beginning of a military campaign. The setting was sumptuous: standards and pennants streamed in the wind from the foot of the terrace; orchestras, consisting mainly of sets of musical stones and golden bells, were grouped near the galleries. Three flights of marble steps lead up the terrace; in the middle of the central flight is a carved marble ramp, over which the emperor's sedan chair was carried.

(*overleaf*) Terrace and gateway leading to the Hall of Perfect Harmony, where the emperor made final preparations before going into the Hall of Supreme Harmony. The finishing touches were given to the message to be read in the Temple of the Ancestors, and once a year the seed for the new sowing was examined here.

Peking. Imperial Palace Museum: exhibition of life-size terracotta figurines made 2,200 years ago to guard the tomb of the first Emperor of China, Qin Shi Huang Di.

> *The war-chariots rattle,*
> *The war-horses whinny.*
> *Each man of you has a bow and a quiver at his belt.*
> *Father, mother, son, wife, stare at you going.*
> *Till dust shall have buried the bridge beyond Chang An.*
> *They run with you, crying, they tug at your sleeves,*
> *And the sound of their sorrow goes up to the clouds;*
> *And every time a bystander asks you a question,*
> *You can only say to him that you have to go . . .*

—From Du Fu (712–770), "A Song of War Chariots,"
translated by Witter Bynner

Peking. Imperial Palace Museum: circular exit from the last of the three halls north of the Gate of the Culture of Character, where some of the old imperial treasures are now exhibited. In former times the apartments of Emperor Qian Long and the Dowager Empress Ci Xi were here. The old Emperor died here on February 17, 1799. It is said that the Dowager hid her casket of jewelry here in 1900 and found it intact on her return.

Peking. Tien An Men, or the Square of the Gate of Heavenly Peace. The square
lies south of the Imperial City, in the center of Peking. It did not exist at the time
of the empire; ministries and offices stood here, among them the Ministries of
Rites, Works, and War and the Astronomical Office. The buildings suffered
damage in 1860 and 1900, and the area slowly widened into a square. In 1912,
after the fall of the empire, the government of the republic used the palace for a
while. The inhabitants of Peking started to gather in the square whenever they
wanted to protest against the government's policies. On October 1, 1949, Chairman Mao Zedong hoisted the red flag with five stars and proclaimed the establish-
ment of the People's Republic of China.

(*above*) Tien An Men Square, looking toward the southern wall of the Imperial
City, with the Gate of Heavenly Peace in the center. Above it, portrait of Mao
Zedong; left and right, the galleries from which leaders and important guests
watch parades.

(*opposite*) The Monument to the People's Heroes in the center of Tien An Men
Square, site of the "Zhou Enlai incident" in 1976, when thousands of people
gathered in open defiance of the Gang of Four. It was this incident that finally
paved the way for the arrest of the Gang of Four by Hua Guofeng's government.
In the background Mao Zedong's mausoleum.

Peking. Old-style house in the western part of town.

(*overleaf*) Peking, near the Drum Tower. Inner garden with fountain.

Lan Xiang Cheng is a learned man, he loves to write verse and drink wine, and, above all, he loves landscapes with mountains and rivers. In his earlier days he was a high official, then he retired and built himself a garden in a beautiful landscape with mountains and water. In the garden he built a study and then he named the study. It was called "Study containing Spring." Some people asked him why he chose this name. He said: I like springtime the best. But it lasts only such a short moment, I want to retain it, I particularly want the inside of my study to be like a very long Spring. So I named it "Study containing Spring."

Peking. Gate and decorative wall surrounding an inner courtyard with a garden giving access to the house, which was formerly owned by a wealthy official.

Peking. On and around Chang An Avenue, from early morning to late at night, people are busy pushing and pulling a multitude of things, often using ingenious homemade devices.

(*preceding spread*) Peking. West Chang An Avenue, 6:30 a.m.

Peking. Encounters in the narrow side streets—called Hu Tung—of the city. A
man from Hebei Province explains how happy he is now that he can live with his
son in Peking. He saw us stop at the entrance to his house and came out to greet
us. At another corner, a young woman stops her bicycle for a conversation with
a friend.

(*opposite*) Peking. Wang Fujing Street, the city's main shopping thoroughfare. A barber uses a long duster made of colored feathers to get his shopwindow shining.

(*below*) Eager customers line up in front of a bookstore offering a number of new titles (translations as well as new editions of Chinese literary works) that for a long time were not only unavailable but indeed forbidden. Available titles are chalked on a blackboard hanging against wall in background.

Peking. Wang Fujing Street, Sunday morning. Cheerful crowds of shoppers
stream out of an indoor market, carrying their purchases in nets, and either pack
them, wrapped in big lotus leaves, onto the backs of their bicycles, or, in the case
of live geese and ducks, wrap their arms happily around them.
(*opposite*) Interior of one of the ubiquitous sweetshops. Opening early and
closing late, they offer a great variety of candy, syrups, cookies, etc.

(*opposite*) Shopwindow of a hatter in Hangzhou, offering all kinds of headgear, from the classic blue cotton cap to Russian-style fur hats, and even something resembling a deerstalker.
(*below*) Peking. Double Bridge People's Commune general store. Display of kitchenware.

Peking. The Summer Palace is located about six miles northwest of Peking, and got its name because the court came here to avoid the heat. In 1153, the Jin Emperor Wan Yanliang built the first palace here, the Garden of Golden Waters. Under the Yuan (1280–1368), the engineer Guo Shoujing enlarged the lake and made the Jade Fountain and the Chang Ping Springs flow into it. The Ming emperors (1368–1644) built the Temple of Perfect Calm and several pavilions. Emperor Qian Long (1736–96) undertook the most extensive work. For his mother's sixtieth birthday he transformed several spots to look like some of the places she had most liked in Hangzhou, and gave the hill its present name of Longevity Hill. The gardens were opened to the public for the first time in 1924, then closed once more by Jiang Qing during the Cultural Revolution in the 1960's. The park has been greatly restored since 1949, and is now one of the most beautiful and frequented spots in the environs of Peking.

(*opposite*) View of Kun Ming Lake.

(*above*) Looking out onto Kun Ming Lake from the covered way linking the buildings scattered from east to west along the shore.

(*overleaf*) Summer Palace: view of Kun Ming Lake. In the background, the magnificent seventeen-arch bridge built to link Long Wang Miao Island with the mainland.

Peking. Chang An Avenue: wall poster on Peace Wall. A great number of the best known and most influential wall posters are put up here. The people of Peking watch this place avidly. On one evening, when a new poster was put up, hundreds of people suddenly gathered in front of the wall and filed past it, reading silently and intently. The next morning, when this picture was taken, and for days to come, the crowd was still silently reading as it filed past the thousands of characters in a slow stream.

(*overleaf*) Interview with actor-director Jin Shan. Foreground: actress Zheng Zenyao; center: Jin Shan.

We had been talking for about an hour now and I needed a couple of minutes to reorganize; for I realized that without planning to I had come to China, a one-party state, poorly prepared by time spent in the Soviet Union, Czechoslovakia, Poland, and Hungary. Of course these people too were hewing to a line—the villainies of the Gang of Four. But I had been in the Soviet Union in the mid-sixties during the "de-Stalinization" time, and Russians even then did not half so openly and self-assuredly tell of sufferings the dictator had caused. His very name was still uneasily spoken and not without a certain psychological glance over the shoulder, quite as though he might rise from his grave. They knew, in Russia, that Stalinists still controlled the big jobs and no doubt the police. And in China too the adherents of the Four had by no means been cleaned out of public life. Was this outspoken interview with me part of the struggle to prevent their enemies from regrouping? I thought so. Rewi Alley had said that many Four supporters had been expelled from their jobs and given lesser ones, and he had quoted Mao on how to deal with people whose ideas are wrong: "People are not chives; their heads do not grow back when they are cut off." This interview, then, was part of the ongoing battle.

—From Arthur Miller's text

(*opposite*) Peking. Corner in living room of a member of Double Bridge People's Commune. Pictures of Zhou Enlai, Mao Zedong, Hua Guofeng, Mao receiving Zhou at Peking Airport, and Mao Zedong mausoleum in Tien An Men Square. Tea things, chest of drawers, and typical bamboo chairs.
(*below*) Peking. Double Bridge People's Commune: interior of general store.

(*above*) Peking. Double Bridge People's Commune: resident barefoot doctor in front of medicine chest containing traditional Chinese herbal medicines. He displays the carapace of a cicada, which is used, in powdered form, in certain herbal medicines. Behind him, an acupuncture chart.

(*opposite*) Commune member describing her work. They have 3,600 acres of arable land; there are six production brigades, with sixty-two production teams under them. The big decisions about crops, quotas to be reached, etc., are made at state level. But the practical decisions about how to realize these plans are made in the commune. This one was founded by mutual aid teams in 1958, after the land reform. Communes are political as well as economic organizations, and include some industry, a militia, and commercial trading, besides agriculture. In Double Bridge People's Commune they raise ducks, pigs, and fish, and grow apples, peaches, grapes, and a hundred varieties of vegetables. They harvest two crops annually, one of rice and one of wheat. "We now practice the system: from each according to his ability, to each according to his labor."

(*opposite, top*) Peking. Factory for generators: the plant's propaganda director in the reception room.

(*bottom*) Peking. Factory for generators: machine room.

(*below*) Peking. Fine arts factory: young women carving intricate statuary in bone. In this factory old and young artisan-artists create some of the most lovely things I have ever seen: carvings in ivory and jade, lacquered objects, cloisonné vases, underglass paintings, even tiny colored figures made out of bread dough. In the jade and coral room each worker works on his or her own piece from beginning to end, even if it takes a year. Using small electric drills over which water is dripped, they produce miraculously delicate chains of jade, lacelike bottles and pendants, and miniature coral trees.

(*preceding spread*) Ming Tomb Alley near Peking. Corpses were carried over this four-mile-long Way of the Spirit. Statues of animals and mandarins, dating from the fifteenth century, line the Sacred Way.

(*below*) Inside the Ming tombs near Peking. The mausoleum was built between 1584 and 1588 for the Emperor Wan Li. It cost 8,000,000 ounces of silver. Wan Li, his empress, Xiao Duan, and his secondary wife, the Empress Xiao Jing, are buried here. Two guardians stand in front of the three altars in the central chamber. In front of each altar is a huge vase with a blue design; these were "eternal lamps," filled with oil to feed the eternal flame.

(*opposite*) Ming Tomb Museum: copy of the Empress's "Phoenix Crown," with dragons and phoenixes. The upper part is made of kingfisher feathers.

The Great Wall of China, or the "Long Wall of 10,000 Li." Three hundred thousand men worked for ten years to carry out this grandiose plan of China's first Emperor, Qin Shi Huang Di.

After this the First Emperor arose to carry on the glorious achievements of six generations. Cracking his long whip, he drove the universe before him, swallowing up the eastern and western Zhou and overthrowing the feudal lords. He ascended to the highest position and ruled the six directions, scouring the world with his rod, and his might shook the four seas. In the south he seized the land of Yueh and made of it the Cassia Forest and Elephant commanderies, and the hundred lords of Yueh bowed their heads, hung halters from their necks, and pleaded for their lives with the lowest officials of Qin. Then he caused Meng Tien to build the Great Wall and defend the borders, driving back the Xiung-nu over seven hundred li so that the barbarians no longer dared to come south to pasture their horses and their men dared not take up their bows to avenge their hatred.

—From Chia Yi, "The Faults of Qin," translated by Burton Watson

Yanan in northern Shaanxi is the place of honor of the Chinese Revolution. In October 1935 the Central Red Army, under command of Mao Zedong, completed the famous "25,000 Li Long March," arriving victorious in northern Shaanxi. Between January 1937 and March 1947 Yanan was the seat of the Central Committee of the Chinese Communist Party, headed by Chairman Mao. From here he led the army and the people in the great War of Resistance against Japan, and in the War of Liberation. Here, too, he wrote many of his works. Zhou Enlai and Zhu De were among the leading figures of the Yanan period. Yanan already had a long revolutionary tradition even before the Communist armies arrived. The town was heavily bombed by the Japanese, and even abandoned for a short time when the Guo Mindang threat became too serious. It was then that Mao Zedong proclaimed the famous slogan: "To keep Yanan is to lose Yanan. To lose Yanan is to keep Yanan."

(*below*) Entrance to cave dwellings inhabited by Mao Zedong, 1938–43.

(*opposite*) Yanan. Entrance to a house, with a string of hot red peppers hung out to dry.

(*above*) Yanan. Revolutionary Museum: in a glass case, the pony Chairman Mao rode during the Long March. On wall in background, photograph of Chairman Mao at work on his writing in Yanan.

(*opposite*) Bedroom in Chairman Mao's last cave residence.

> *All these appealing charms of hill and stream*
> *Made jealous suitors out of countless heroes.*
> *But the first Emperor or Wu of the Han*
> *Could boast of few refinements,*
> *The founders of Tang or Song*
> *Lacked elegance,*
> *And one who lorded it across an age,*
> *Genghis Khan,*
> *Had no art but to draw his bow at eagles.*
> *All went their way:*
> *The search for true nobility*
> *Waits on our time.*

—From Mao Zedong, "Snow," translated by Cyril Birch

(*above*) Yanan, Yan River: hauling loess from riverbed for building material.

> *In the areas watered by the Yellow River*
> *In the countless dry riverbeds*
> *Wheelbarrows*
> *With their single wheel*
> *Give out squeaks that make the cloudy sky contract*
> *Pass through the cold and the silence*
> *From the foot of this hill*
> *To the foot of that hill*
> *Crying aloud*
> *The gloom of the people of the North.*

—From Ai Quing (b. 1910), "The Wheelbarrows," translated by
Tao Tao Sanders

(*opposite*) Nanniwan, Shaanxi Province. May 7 Cadre School: carpenter shop.

Nanniwan, Shaanxi Province. Hulling rice at May 7 Cadre School. The name of these schools is derived from Mao Zedong's "May 7 Directive," which asked all cadres to take part in manual labor. This directive was issued during the Cultural Revolution; the school in Nanniwan was set up in 1968. Nanniwan itself, however, had ties with Yanan during the revolutionary period (the Eighth Route Army was stationed here from 1941). Later it became an artillery school. Since the soldiers cultivated the land, Nanniwan was abandoned when the army marched on Peking. When the first cadres arrived, they found only wasteland. At first they lived in tents, building everything themselves. Now there are pigsties and farmyards with chickens, geese, ducks, and cows. There are 800 *mu* (a *mu* is equal to about one sixth of an acre) of cultivated land, 177 cave dwellings, and 132 new homes. The head of the school told us about the "Repudiate the Bourgeoisie" movement in 1968–69, during the Great Cultural Revolution. Many people came to the country to work, including cadres, heads of workshops, factories, and so on; their main aims were to study important principles, work in agriculture, and carry on the Yanan spirit of self-reliance.

(*opposite*) View of Xian, the capital of Shaanxi Province, from the belltower, which, during the Tang period, stood in the middle of the Imperial City. It was dismantled and moved to its present location in 1582, to be once again at the center of the town's north-south axis. High roof on right is Drum Tower, built in 1370, under the Ming emperors. Xian is an ancient city. From the eleventh century B.C. it was the capital city of eleven dynasties. Its first great period was under the first Emperor, Qin Shi Huang Di, who enlarged the town after the unification of his empire.

Qin Shi Huang Di moved as many as 120 families to Xian Yang, rich and powerful men from all over the empire . . . Every time Qin overcame a prince, he copied the plan of his palace and had it rebuilt in Xian Yang. From Yong Men going east as far as the rivers Jing and Wei, the buildings, dwellings, covered ways and arcades touched each other. Everything that Qin Shi Huang Di took from the lords such as beautiful women, bells and drums, he ordered to be put in his palaces, which were full of them . . .

—From *Historical Records of Si ma qien*, translated by E. Chavannes

Xian's golden age of art and literature came under the Tang emperors (A.D. 618–906), when the city bore the name Chang An.

(*preceding spread*) View of Hua Qing Springs, at the foot of the Li Shan hills. The emperors loved to bathe here. Residences were built, legends were born. The most famous of these legends was the tragic love of Emperor Xuan Zong and his concubine Yang Guifei, immortalized in Po Qu Yi's "Song of Unending Sorrow."

Hua Qing Springs, Shaanxi Province. Hua Qing Springs was also the scene of a famous incident in more recent times. The "Xian incident" took place here in 1936. Chiang Kai-shek was taken prisoner by his own deputy commander-in-chief, Marshal Chang Xue-liang, in a final attempt to force him to join the Communist forces in a united front. The visitor can retrace the Generalissimo's steps from his bedroom (*above*) to the window from which he jumped, his barefoot flight up the steps, over a wall, and across a stony slope to the place of his capture by a soldier (*opposite*).

Xian. Shaanxi Provincial Museum. (*above*) Hall of ancient stone sculptures, many of them animals from imperial tombs dating from the Han, Wei, and Tang dynasties. (*opposite*) Three wooden sculptures in former Buddhist temple. The museum is rich in treasures from the past, among them the "forest of tablets," a library in stone. There are over 1,000 stones, the best of which date from the Tang dynasty; 114 of them are engraved with the 50,000 characters making up the text of the Twelve Classics.

(*overleaf*) Lin Tong, Shaanxi Province. Terracotta figures, part of an army of 6,000 life-size statues now being excavated in one of the greatest archaeological finds of this century. They guarded the still-closed tomb of China's first Emperor, Qin Shi Huang Di. An immense museum is being built on the site to house this army, now restored to its original formation.

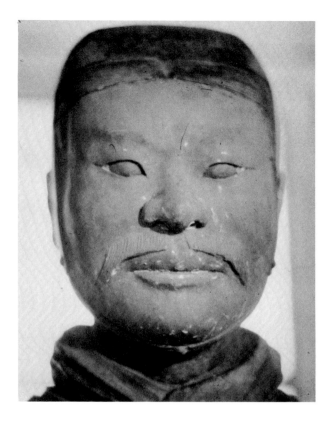

Qin Shi Huang Di started building his tomb at the beginning of his reign (229–201 B.C.).

The workmen sent there numbered over seven hundred thousand. They dug down as far as the water; bronze was poured and the sarcophagus brought . . . marvelous tools, jewels and rare objects were brought there and buried . . . Artisans were ordered to make automatic crossbows and arrows; if anyone had tried to make a hole and enter the tomb, they would have immediately fired on him. The hundred water courses, the Yangtze, the He and the vast sea were represented by quicksilver; machines made it run and carried it from one to another. All signs of the heavens were above, and the geographical arrangement below . . .

The emperor ordained that all his wives should follow him when he died . . . When the work was over and the central passage leading to the tomb had been disguised and blocked, the outer door to it was dropped into place, shutting in all those who had been employed as workmen or craftsmen . . . Plants and grass were planted so that the tomb looked like a hill.

—From *Historical Records of Si ma qien*, translated by E. Chavannes

(opposite) Pools and pavilions at Hua Qing Springs Park.

China's Emperor, craving beauty that might shake an empire,
Was on the throne, for many years, searching, never finding,
Till a little child of the Yang clan, hardly even grown,
Bred in an inner chamber, with no one knowing her,
But with graces granted by heaven and not to be concealed,
At last one day was chosen for the imperial household.
If she but turned her head and smiled, there were cast a
    hundred spells,
And the powder and paint of the Six Palaces faded into nothing.
. . . It was early spring. They bathed her in the Flower-Pure Pool,
Which warmed and smoothed the creamy-tinted crystal of her skin,
    and, because of her languor, a maid was lifting her
When first the Emperor noticed her and chose her for his bride.
The cloud of her hair, petal of her cheek, gold ripples of her
    crown when she moved,
Were sheltered on spring evenings by warm hibiscus-curtains;
But nights of spring were short and the sun arose too soon,
And the Emperor, from that time forth, forsook his early hearings
And lavished all his time on her with feasts and revelry,
His mistress of the spring, his despot of the night.

The Emperor's eyes could never gaze on her enough—
Till war-drums, booming from Yuyang, shocked the whole earth . . .
The Forbidden city, the nine-tiered palace, loomed in the dust
From thousands of horses and chariots headed southwest.
The imperial flag opened the way, now moving and now pausing—
But thirty miles from the capital, beyond the western gate,
The men of the army stopped, not one of them would stir
Till under their horses' hoofs they might trample those
    moth-eyebrows . . .
Flowery hairpins fell to the ground, no one picked them up,
And a green and white jade hair-tassel and a yellow-gold hair-bird.
The Emperor could not save her, he could only cover his face.
And later when he turned to look, the place of blood and tears
Was hidden in a yellow dust blown by a cold wind.

And when heaven and earth resumed their round and the dragon car
    faced home,
The Emperor clung to the spot and would not turn away
From the soil along the Mawei slope, under which was buried
That memory, that anguish. Where was her jade-white face?
. . . The pools, the gardens, the palace, all were just as before,
The Lake Tai Ye hibiscus, the Weiyang Palace willows;
But a petal was like her face and a willow-leaf her eyebrow—
And what could he do but cry whenever he looked at them?

—From Po Qu Yi (772–844), "A Song of Unending Sorrow," translated by
    Witter Bynner

Nanjing, capital of Jiangsu Province: the Yangtze River and the great Yangtze River bridge. The bridge is a double-decker rail and highway bridge, designed and built entirely by the Chinese people. Linking the north and the south banks of the Yangtze River, it has an important role in the modernization of socialist China. Mao Zedong swam across the Yangtze in 1956, at the age of sixty-three. He commemorated the event in the following poem, which at the same time celebrates the marvelous construction feat of his new regime, the great bridge.

> *Wind-sway of masts*
> *Repose of Tortoise and Snake*
> *And a great plan begun:*
> *A single span to soar*
> *North-south thoroughfare over nature's moat.*

—From Mao Zedong, "Swimming," translated by Cyril Birch

Nanjing. One of China's ancient capitals, with a history going back 2,400 years, it was a center not only of feudal but also of modern revolutionary activities. The "Taiping heavenly kingdom," a mid-nineteenth-century peasant revolutionary movement, made its center here. In 1912 Sun Yat-sen was elected President of the new Republic in Nanjing. His rule was followed by Chiang Kai-shek's repressive Guo Mindang regime. The Japanese occupied the city for many years during the War of Resistance. Since Liberation, Nanjing has developed rapidly, especially in industrial and agricultural production.

(*above*) Nanjing, Xuan Wu Lake Park. Youngsters enjoying the October 1 holiday.

(*opposite, top*) Nanjing. Mausoleum of Sun Yat-sen.

(*bottom*) Nanjing. Statue of Sun Yat-sen near the foot of the huge flight of steps that lead up to the mausoleum.

Nanjing has always been an important economic center, famous for its forges and foundries, its weaving, and its pottery kilns. Its long artistic and scientific tradition lives on in its institutions of higher learning, and in the famous Purple Mountain Observatory, one of the largest in China.

(*opposite, top*) Nanjing fruit stall.

(*bottom*) Bookshop with clerk pointing out newly issued editions of Chinese literature.

(*overleaf*) Nanjing. Sacred Way to the mausoleum of Emperor Hong Wu.

> *I'm a won't-soften-when-you-steam-me never-ready-when-*
> *   you-boil-me pounding-won't-flatten-me frying-won't-cook-*
> *   me dingdong ringing copper pea.*
> *Youngsters, who was it taught you to drill*
> *Those hoes-won't-slice-them hatchets-won't-crack-them*
> *   won't-be-wrenched-open won't-be-worked-loose maddening*
> *   boxes within boxes inside the brocade box?*
> *I play with the moon on the Liang Terrace,*
> *Drink the wine of the East Capital,*
> *Fancier of Luoyang flowers,*
> *Plucker of willows on the Chang Terrace.*
> *I, too, can play chess like you, play football, beat for the*
> *   hunters, mime on the stage, sing and dance, blow and*
> *   strum, chant verses, play backgammon . . .*
> *You have made me toothless, wrymouthed,*
> *Lamed my legs, cracked my knuckles,*
> *Heaven's gifts to me are all these wretched ills,*
> *And still I'm the one man who doesn't give up.*

—From Guan Han-qing (ca. 1220–ca. 1300), "Defy Old Age," *Song Set*, translated by A. C. Graham

(*opposite*) Tomb in a hillside, Guangxi Zhuang Autonomous Region.
(*above*) Nanjing. Farmer plowing just outside the town.
(*overleaf*) Yangtze River Valley landscape. Main crops are rice and wheat, tea, vegetables, apples, cherries, and watermelons.

> *In the sixth month we eat wild plums and cherries,*
> *In the seventh month we boil mallows and beans.*
> *In the eighth month we dry the dates,*
> *In the tenth month we take the rice*
> *To make with it the spring wine,*
> *So that we may be granted long life.*
> *In the seventh month we eat melons,*
> *In the eighth month we cut the gourds,*
> *In the ninth month we take the seeding hemp,*
> *We gather bitter herbs, we cut the ailanto for firewood,*
> *That our husbandmen may eat.*
>
> —From *The Book of Songs* (Chou dynasty), translated by Arthur Waley

Shanghai. District in the north section of the "old town," formerly also called the "Chinese town," which was still surrounded by walls at the beginning of this century. It was roughly round and had a circumference of two or three miles. The streets are centered around a small lake, with a teahouse in the middle.
(*above*) Old town. Lake in front of the "Mandarin Yu's Garden." Shanghai boatwoman glides past "the Pavilion that receives the moonlight first."
(*opposite*) Street in the old town. In bygone days foreigners were warned against entering here without a Chinese guide. A stroll through the impeccably clean streets today is only a partial reminder of an older China, without a trace of the old plagues of starvation, prostitution, and general depravity.
(*preceding spread*) Street in old town. The pointed roof (background, right) belongs to the old teahouse, which was Shanghai's symbol and reproduced on plates and curios.

Shanghai began as a fishing village and was a flourishing harbor by the seventeenth century. After 1853 it was controlled by the Western colonial powers, and became an "adventurers' paradise," while the majority of the Chinese population was plagued with endless ills and misery. Shanghai has a great revolutionary tradition, and since the Liberation has become an important industrial center, and a focus for science and culture, while retaining its role as one of China's major international trading ports. The city already has 10,000,000 inhabitants, and in an attempt to slow down its growth, several satellite towns have been founded nearby. These developments are self-contained communities whose economic centers are the new industrial plants. Workers and their families live in apartments in three- or four-story blocks, within walking distance of their work. There are small gardens, playgrounds, nurseries, schools, general stores, sometimes truck farms, pigsties, and poultry yards owned and managed by the factories.

(*opposite*) Shanghai workers' housing development. Woman in her bed-sitting room.

(*below*) Shanghai workers' housing development. Workshop organized by housewives to "make their socialist contribution." They process, calibrate, polish, and pack medical glassware.

Shanghai. Cao Yang II middle school: daily eye exercises, and a pupil preparing to answer a question in a mathematics class. The school has 1,600 pupils, who attend six classes daily. Subjects are political science, Chinese, foreign languages including English, mathematics, physics, biology, chemistry, history, geography, music, and fine arts. Two weeks a term pupils work in school-connected factories. After the second class in the afternoon they can choose among the free occupations, which are dance, painting, construction of model boats and airplanes, studying a homemade seismograph, or working out on the sports grounds. During the Cultural Revolution the school practically came to a standstill, no exams were held, and all labs were closed. Whoever sat it out got promoted. "Some," said one of the political advisers, "carried on with their studies anyway, but secretly." Now all is back to normal, the students seem eager and motivated, and the slogan on the wall in back of the classroom reads: "Sound body, good study, good work."

The history of Shanghai's domination by foreigners, like its revolutionary tradition, is a long one. In the nineteenth century the West took over the city's development after Shanghai's surrender at the end of the Opium Wars. The English, French, Americans, and, finally, Japanese claimed their special territories, the notorious "concessions." In 1853 the Taiping revolutionaries got as far as the outskirts of Shanghai, though they were then put down, with European help, by the imperial armies. The "Society of Little Swords" planned an uprising in the town itself at the same time. The Chinese Communist Party was founded on July 1, 1921, in Shanghai, which was the seat of the Party's Central Committee for some time. Working-class armed uprisings were savagely put down by Chiang Kai-shek after 1927. Shanghai was occupied by the Japanese during the Sino-Japanese war. Since Liberation, Shanghai has become a different city; the Europeans have gone, and with them the contrasts of immense wealth cheek-by-jowl with naked starvation, prostitution, gangsters, opium dens, beggars, and corpses in the streets.

(*above*) First meeting place of the Central Committee of the Chinese Communist Party.

(*opposite*) Corner in room of Shanghai house where Sun Yat-sen and his wife, Soong Chingling, lived.

Shanghai. Living room in house of Lu Xun, one of China's most famous writers and essayists and an innovator in the use of the spoken language (*bai hua*) in literature. He died here in 1936. His portrait is on the wall. His literary work, mostly short stories and essays, was written to arouse the spirit of his countrymen. "I felt . . . that I should write in the hope of enlightening my people, for humanity, and of the need to better it. I detested the old notion of fiction as 'entertainment' and regarded 'art for art's sake' as simply a synonym for wasting time. So my themes were usually the unfortunates in this abnormal society. My aim was to expose the disease and draw attention to it, so that it might be cured." Lu Xun took an active part in the 1919 May 4 movement, a mass revolt of students and intellectuals against the Treaty of Versailles in particular and imperialism and feudalism in general. He was a teacher and regarded his art as "merely a social phenomenon, a record of the times." Most of his work consists of polemical essays, masterpieces of innuendo and allusion, since they had to get past the censor. His first published book was *A Madman's Diary*, one of the most important events in modern Chinese literary history.

One of Lu Xun's masterpieces is *The True Story of Ah Q*, which is about a rather disreputable peasant living by his wits in the semifeudal society at the time of the 1911 Revolution.

For a couple of years I have been wanting to write the true story of Ah Q, but while on the one hand I was desirous of doing it, on the other I vacillated in my purpose. This proves that I am not the person who can depend upon his writing to preserve his name, because in times past it has been necessary that an immortal pen preserve the memory of a person destined for imperishable fame; therefore, it is not clear which is dependent upon the other, whether the person is propagated by the pen, or the pen by the person . . .

To settle the matter once and for all we might consider this a personal record; but using my own way of writing which is in the language of wagon-haulers and street-mongers and very inferior and unseemly.

—From Lu Xun, *The True Story of Ah Q*

Mao Zedong held Lu Xun, who used literature as his weapon, in high esteem: "The chief commander of China's cultural revolution, he [Lu Xun] was not only a great man of letters, but a great thinker and revolutionary." (*On New Democracy*, 1940)

(*overleaf*) Shanghai. Dividing wall carved in the shape of a dragon. Yu Yuan, a garden laid out in 1537 by a Ming dynasty official who subsequently lived there. (*overleaf, second spread*) Shanghai. Inside one of the pavilions in the Yu Yuan is a small museum of the Society of Little Swords, containing all kinds of memorabilia, including swords worn by members of the society and a plan of their siege of Shanghai.

Shanghai. The huge Palace of Sino-Soviet Friendship houses the permanent exhibition of products manufactured in the city, including machines, cars, trucks, precision tools, consumer goods, lighting equipment, crafts, and textiles. (*above*) A guide explains the workings of a new mechanical loom.
(*opposite*) Along the waterfront near the Bund, people pose in front of a new poster urging the Chinese to modernize their country by the year 2000.

Hangzhou, capital of Zhejiang Province. Over 2,000 years old, it lies on the northern bank of the Jien Tang River and borders on the celebrated West Lake. From the visit of Emperor Qin Shi around 200 B.C. through the dynasties of the Sui, Tang, and Song, rivers were dammed, causeways and canals built, houses and palaces erected. In 1270 about 900,000 people lived in Hangzhou. In the thirteenth century, Marco Polo wrote after visiting Hangzhou:

. . . There is always an ample supply of every kind of meat and game, and an infinite quantity of duck and geese . . . from the ocean sea come daily supplies of fish in great quantity . . . all the ten market places are encompassed by lofty houses, and below these are the shops where all sorts of crafts are carried on, and all sorts of wares are on sale, including spices and jewels and pearls.

—From *Ser Marco Polo concerning the Kingdoms and Marvels of the East,* translated and edited by Sir Henry Yule

(*preceding 2 spreads*) Hangzhou region. Members of Mei Jia Wu tea production brigade picking Long Jing cha, one of China's most famous green teas. Mei Jia Wu village: reception room of the tea production brigade in house of a former landlord, still furnished with Ming chairs and tables.

(*above*) Hangzhou, Tiger Spring. Delicate screen in front of a tearoom.
(*right*) Marine posing with symbol of Tiger Spring, whose water is the best for brewing the famous Long Jing tea, grown in this region.

(*opposite*) Mei Jia Wu village, Hangzhou region. Old man looking after his grandson.

> *Mat over mat, bamboo on rush*
> *so it be soft, to sleep, to wake in hush,*
> *from dreams of bears and snakes?*
> > *Saith the diviner:*
>
> *Which mean*
> *Bears be for boys; snakes, girls.*
> *Boys shall have beds, hold sceptres for their toys,*
> *creep on red leather,*
> *bellow when they would cry*
> *in embroidered coats,*
> *ere come to Empery.*
>
> *Small girls shall sleep on floor and play with tiles,*
> *wear simple clothes and do no act amiss,*
> *cook, brew and seemly speak,*
> *conducing so the family's quietness.*

—From *The Book of Songs* (Chou dynasty), translated by Ezra Pound

Hangzhou. Silk mill: spinning thread, mending tiny faults, transferring new patterns onto cards, and (*overleaf*) creating a new woven silk image of Chairman Hua Guofeng. Hangzhou's silk filatures are flourishing. They produce a startling array of lovely satins, silks, brocades, woven silk pictures, even parasols made of silk. Other local products are sandalwood fans, chopsticks, little knives. Besides the famous green tea, the region grows cotton, hemp, and rice, and raises silkworms.

Hangzhou. Pavilions overlooking West Lake.

I always remember West Lake—
On the lake, when spring comes, there's an endless view:
The girls of Wu, every single one a goddess,
Vying with one another in rowing their magnolia boats.

Clusters of pavilions and towers that look like the Magic Isle—
There and only there should a rustic grow old.
Since I left, it's been twenty years already.
Gazing eastward, my eyes will soon wear out.

—From Pan Lang (A.D. 1009?), "Tune of the Wine Spring,"
translated by James J. Y. Liu

(*overleaf*) Hangzhou. Bas-relief of a Buddha.

"The Peak which flew here," a hillside opposite the Ling Yin Si temple. The temple was founded in the fourth century by Hui Li, who arrived from India and, when he saw the hill, claimed to recognize it as a corner of Mount Grdhrakuta "which had flown here." The temple was destroyed and rebuilt several times. The rock carvings date from the end of the thirteenth and the beginning of the fourteenth centuries, and represent one of the rare surviving examples of Yuan rock sculpture.

(*opposite*) Hangzhou. Interior of Ling Yin Si temple. Restored since the Liberation, it contains large Buddhas and a group of Luo Han made of gilded clay. Huge red lacquered columns on round stone bases support the carved ceiling.

Next we climbed to the Chamber of Guan Yin;
From afar we sniffed its odours of sandal-wood.
At the top of the steps each doffed his shoes;
With bated stride we crossed the Jasper Hall.
The Jewelled Mirror on six pillars propped . . .
When the wind came jewels chimed and sang
Softly, softly like the music of Paradise.
White pearls like frozen dewdrops hanging,
Dark rubies spilt like clots of blood,
Spangled and sown on the Buddha's twisted hair,
Together fashioned his Sevenfold Jewel-crown.
In twin vases of pallid tourmaline
(Their colour colder than the waters of an autumn stream)
The calcined relics of Buddha's Body rest—
Rounded pebbles, smooth as the Specular Stone.
A jade flute, by angels long ago
Borne as a gift to the Garden of Jetavan!
It blows a music sweet as the crane's song
That Spirits of Heaven earthward well might draw.

—From Po Qu Yi (772–846), "The Temple," translated by Arthur Waley

(*opposite*) Arthur Miller and interpreter Su Guang at the foot of a Yuan dynasty sculpture of a Vajrapani, or defender of Buddhism, at the approach to the "Peak that flew here," and only a few miles from West Lake and its "Broken Bridge," where much of the action of the opera *The White Snake* takes place.

(*overleaf*) Two of the demons sent by Abbot Fa Hai of Golden Mountain Monastery to capture the White Snake Spirit, as they appeared in a Shanghai production of the famous old opera.

A thousand years ago in Sichuan Province, where, just as today, the E Mei Mountain stands, a magnet for all sorts of fairy folk, the snake fairy Bai Si Jian, the White Snake, descended from heaven . . . She was accompanied by her sister, the Green Snake, or Little Green Snake . . .

White Snake and sister arrive in Zhejiang Province near Hangzhou at the shore of West Lake . . . It starts to rain and they naturally look around for somebody who will lend them an umbrella. In their search they run into an umbrella owner named Xue Xien, whom, after carefully considering him for an aria, the White Snake decides to marry.

—From Arthur Miller's text

Guilin, Guangxi Zhuang Autonomous Region. The town lies on the upper reaches of the river Li. It was founded in 214 B.C., under Qin Shi Huang Di. Now a growing industrial town, Guilin is famous for its superb landscapes. The underlying rock here is limestone, and natural erosion has produced a scenery full of fantastic shapes. Countless poets and artists have been attracted by the strange summits rising from the plains bordering on the Li and Gui Rivers, and there are many legends concerning their origins, as well as those of the town. When Guilin was still surrounded by wild untamed countryside, demons, giant snakes, and fierce beasts used to come and seize people's possessions. One day the sky suddenly grew dark, a violent wind blew up, and a giant demon could be seen far off, leaning against the "hill with a hole through it" (*Chuan shan*). His hands looked like dragon's claws, and in each one he held a boa spitting poisonous vapors. At that moment a thunderclap was heard on Fu Bo Shan hill, and a giant appeared in a blaze of light. He was over ten feet high and carried a huge bow. A great sword hung at his side, his eyes flashed lightning, and he spoke in ringing tones. His name was Jie Di. He took his bow and with one arrow killed the monster and pierced the mountain through. The other demons and fierce animals fled, terrified, never to return, and from that day on the people of Guilin lived in peace.

(*opposite*) Guilin. The Returned Pearl Cave on the south slope of Fu Bo Shan hill. One of the walls of the cave has an engraving by Song painter Mi Wan Gong, who was an official in Guilin.

(*overleafs*) Guilin. Street scenes: young student reading in front of his house, in an older part of the town near the Li River. Bookshop on main street, and a sampling of the methods used to transport oneself and one's load.

(*opposite*) Landscape with water buffaloes outside Guilin. Most of the population of this area belongs to the Zhuang minority. The main crops are rice, sweet potatoes, sugar cane, and grapefruit. Star anise, cinnamon, and tea oil are also produced. Frequent fires have destroyed most of the original forest, and now efforts are being made to build reservoirs to hold the water, which otherwise seeps away through the limestone rocks.

Speed, speed the plow
on south slopes now
grain is to sow
    lively within.

Here come your kin,
baskets round
baskets square,
millet's there.

With a crowd of rain-hats
and clicking hoes
out goes the weed
to mulch and rot
or dry and wet,
crop will be thicker on that spot.

Harvest high,
reapers come by
so they mow
to heap it like a wall
comb-tooth'd and tall.

an hundred barns to fill
till wives and childer fear no ill.

At harvest home kill a yellow bull,
by his curved horn is luck in full
(be he black-nosed seven feet high,
so tall's felicity).

Thus did
men of old
who left us this land
to have and to hold.

—From *The Book of Songs* (Chou dynasty), translated by Ezra Pound

Guangxi Zhuang Autonomous Region. Peasants on the roads between villages.

Long hoe, long hoe, with your raw wooden handle,
I entrust my life to you, you are my only provider.
The yams have no shoots, the mountain snow is deep.
I pull down my short coat many times; it won't cover my shins.
Today we return empty-handed, you and I;
My son groans, my daughter moans, the four walls are quiet.

Alas! This is my second song, oh! I begin to sing it loud.
My neighbors' faces are distressed on my behalf.

—From Du Fu (712–770), "Seven Songs Written While Living at Tung-ku in 759,"
translated by Geoffrey Waters

Guilin. Courtyard just off the street in the old part of town near the river. In the shed in back of the yard, a carpenter's shop; outside, a pile of boards ready for use. On the left, all kinds of edible plants crowd around and over a tool shed: gourds, corn, peppers, and a couple of small fruit trees.

Guilin. On the banks of the Li River, a man waters his vegetable plot: onions, leeks, cabbages, and melons.

> Lucky to own a melon patch by the Green Gate;
> Who would envy the marquisate of a hundred square miles?
> Watered from the well-pump, leek shoots grow thick and broad.
> How Fan Qih was elated to learn gardening!
> Three cups of wine beneath the pear tree,
> A mat in the shade of willows—
> What unrestrained freedom!
> My meal: a schoolteacher's meager porridge,
> A poor fellow's yellow leek.

[Fan Qih was a disciple of Confucius.]

—From Ma Qih Yuan (1260–1334?), "Slow Chant," translated by Sherwin S. S. Fu

Guangxi Zhuang Autonomous Region. Boat traffic on the Li River. Running through one of the most famous scenic landscapes of China, this river has been celebrated by poets and painters. But it is also a great favorite with fishermen, whose delicate rods, with a rice kernel for bait, stick out from humps of lime-stone in the water, waiting for a bite. Their owners gather water plants in the shallows for fertilizer, or sit on boats made, like flutes, of tied-together bamboo canes. Tiny villages, shaded by extravagant bamboos, are dotted along the banks, and a multicolored, multishaped crowd of boats populates its limpid waters.

(*overleaf*) Boat harbor, Li River, near Guilin.

(*opposite*) Li River landscape.
(*overleaf*) Fishing boat on the Li River.

X

Elongated-like: broken then joined again
Unbending-like: deserting then meeting again

Agape-like: fish mouths gasping from duckweed
Sparse-like: constellations traversed by the moon

Majestic-like: trees tall in the courtyard
Peaked-like: granaries stacked up high

Pointed-like: halberds standing sharp
Glittering-like: holding jade and jasper

Opening-like: flowers unfurling the calyx
Dripping-like: rain falling from broken eaves

Leisure-like: stretched out and calm
Obstinate-like: familiar and pushy

Superior-like: emergent and speeding
Squirming-like: frightened, unwilling to stir.

XI

How large! rising between heaven and earth ,
Their patterns copying the skin's network.

In their beginning, who spread them out?
Who worked, who advised,

Creating them simple and ingenious,
Combining strengths to endure the toil?

Did they use axes to hew,
Or borrow power from magic invocations?

Since nothing is known of the Primal Darkness,
This stately achievement goes unacknowledged.

Learning from the shrine attendant that the mountain spirit
Descended in person to inhale the sacrificial fragrance,

With rhetoric I composed this poem,
Hoping by it to offer my gratitude.

—From Han Yu (768–824), "Southern Mountains," translated by Charles Hartman

(*opposite*) Guilin. The town's big new opera house, a performance of *Sister Liu*, a modern, animated, and successful opera packed with melodies of popular songs. It is the tale of a young peasant girl, Sister Liu, born with a voice and heart of gold, who can't stop singing. She wins out over a great many bad elements, in particular a greedy landlord. In the picture she is with her friends, listening to news brought by a sympathetic fisherman.

(*below*) Guilin. A baby waiting for his father's return, inside the ingenious structure built on top of his motorbike. More ancient, but equally ingenious, is the baby's bamboo stroller-playpen, parked next to the "car."

Guangzhou, capital of Guangdong Province, lies on the Pearl River,
the biggest watercourse in southern China. Foreign influence arrived early; a
mosque was built in the seventh century, and a Portuguese embassy established
in the sixteenth. Many overseas Chinese are from Guangdong. After 1850
Europeans were granted "concessions" and a history of struggle against foreign
rule ensued. Sun Yat-sen, a native of Guangdong, led the Chinese revolution
and founded his Guo Mindang here in 1923. Mao Zedong ran the peasant movement institute here with, among others, Zhou Enlai and Guo Mojo. Today Guangzhou has a population of 2,000,000. Modernized by Sun Yat-sen, it has a budding
metal industry fueled by coal, iron, and non-ferrous metals from its own mines.
Its subtropical climate produces three hundred kinds of fruit, two rice crops,
tobacco, cotton, flax, sisal, coconut, palm oil, and coffee. Silkworms and fish are
raised; the handcrafts are famous.
(*above*) View of the Pearl River from Sha Mian Island.
(*opposite*) Loads of baskets arrive for local stores.

(*above*) Guangzhou. The former Franco-British concession of Sha Mian still has a nineteenth-century colonial air about it. It now houses administrative buildings and some schools. There are pleasant walkways and sports grounds along the tree-shaded embankments.

(*opposite, top*) Sha Mian Island. Future gymnasts and acrobats indulge in a little open-air training.

(*opposite, bottom*) Sha Mian Island. Two workmen chopping up a banyan tree with a handsaw. Behind them some tennis courts.

(*overleaf*) Foshan. Ten miles southwest of Guangzhou. This town used to be an important religious and economic center. The products of its pottery kilns and workshops have been sold all over the world for hundreds of years. The photographs show two details from the Zu Ci Miao Taoist temple in Foshan. Founded under the Ming dynasty, taken over by the Taiping rebels in the nineteenth century, and reconstructed under the Qing, it is now a museum. Detail of woodcarving from an altar screen and sculpture of tortoise and snake.